The Fading Script: Cursive Writing and the Erosion of Our Historical Legacy

Copyright © 2025 All rights reserved.

No portion of this book may be reproduced or transmitted electronically without authorized consent from the author.

ISBN: 979-8-9990071-6-2

Book Summary: *The Fading Script: Cursive Writing and the Erosion of Our Historical Legacy*

In *The Fading Script*, Steve the author weaves a compelling narrative about the rise, fall, and urgent revival of cursive writing in American society. The book begins with the historical roots of cursive, tracing its evolution from ancient scripts to the elegant copperplate handwriting that defined early American documents. It highlights how cursive became a cornerstone of education and communication, enabling fluid expression and personal connection in an era before typewriters and keyboards. Through vivid stories of historical figures from the Founding Fathers drafting the US Constitution in flowing script to everyday citizens penning letters during wars and migrations the book illustrates cursive's role in preserving human stories, legal records, and cultural artifacts.

The core of the story pivots to the modern decline: Starting in the 1970s and accelerating with the 2010 removal of cursive from the Common Core Standards, schools across the US shifted focus to digital literacy and typing skills, deeming handwriting obsolete in a tech-driven world.

Table Of Content

Introduction: The Legacy of Cursive
Chapter 1: The Ancient Roots of Script
Chapter 2: Cursive in the Age of Enlightenment
Chapter 3: The Founding Fathers' Flourish
Chapter 4: Cursive as a Pillar of Education
Chapter 5:Golden Era Handwritten Communication
Chapter 6: The Digital Shift Begins
Chapter 7: Common Core and the Cursive Purge
Chapter 8: The Unreadable Past
Chapter 9: Cognitive Costs of Abandoning Cursive
Chapter 10: Generational Divide
Chapter 11: Global Perspectives on Handwriting
Chapter 12: A Case for Reviving Cursive
Chapter 13: Cursive in the Digital Age
Chapter 14: Ancient Greeks & Birth of Cursive
Chapter 15: A New Era for Cursive
Conclusion: Cursive Future

Introduction: The Legacy of Cursive and the Constitution

In the quiet chambers of Philadelphia in 1787, a group of visionaries gathered to draft a document that would shape the destiny of a young nation. With quills dipped in ink, they penned the United States Constitution, its elegant copperplate script flowing across parchment in a testament to the power of the written word. Each loop, flourish, and carefully formed letter carried the weight of their ideals liberty, justice, and the pursuit of a more perfect union. This cursive script, a hallmark of the era, was not merely a means of communication but a symbol of human thought, connecting the hands of the Founders to the minds of future generations. For centuries, cursive handwriting served as a bridge to this past, enabling Americans to read the Constitution, personal letters, diaries, and deeds that tell the story of who we are. Yet, in the 21st century, this bridge is crumbling. The rise of the digital age, accelerated by educational reforms like the 2010 Common Core Standards, has sidelined cursive in favor of keyboards and touchscreens, leaving a generation unable to decipher the very documents that define their heritage.

This book is a journey through the rise, fall, and potential revival of cursive handwriting in America, a narrative that intertwines the art of penmanship with the nation's identity. It begins in the 19th century, when cursive was a pillar of education, taught in one-room schoolhouses where children copied the Constitution's preamble to learn both writing and citizenship. It traces the golden era of handwritten communication, when letters, ledgers, and legal records, all penned in flowing script, were the lifeblood of a growing nation. As technology advanced, from typewriters to computers, cursive's dominance waned, culminating in the Common Core's cursive purge, which prioritized digital skills over historical literacy. The consequences are profound: students today stand before the Constitution's parchment, its words a mystery, while family heirlooms letters from soldiers, recipes from grandmothers remain locked in unreadable scripts.

The story is not one of loss alone. Across the globe, nations like France and Japan show that cursive, or its equivalents, can thrive alongside technology, preserving access to historical records while fostering cognitive growth. In America, voices from the frontlines teachers, students, parents, and elders call for a revival, sharing stories of disconnection and hope. From classrooms using tablets to teach cursive to communities hosting workshops to decode family archives, a new era for cursive is emerging, one that blends tradition with innovation. This book argues that cursive is not a relic but a vital skill, essential for reading the Constitution, understanding our ancestors, and enriching our minds. It is a call to action, urging us to preserve this bridge to our past before it fades entirely.

The chapters that follow explore this narrative in depth, weaving together history, culture, and science to make a case for cursive's revival. Chapter 4 delves into cursive's role as a pillar of 19th-century education, where students learned to write by copying the Constitution, embedding its ideals in their hands and hearts. Chapter 5 celebrates the golden era of handwritten communication, when cursive letters connected families and communities, mirroring the script of the nation's founding documents. Chapter 6 traces the digital shift, as typewriters and computers began to overshadow penmanship, setting the stage for cursive's decline. Chapter 7 examines the Common Core's cursive purge, a policy that prioritized typing but left students unable to read historical texts. Chapter 8 confronts the unreadable past, illustrating how the loss of cursive creates barriers to archives and personal records. Chapter 9 highlights the cognitive costs, from weakened memory to diminished literacy, while Chapter 10 gathers voices from the frontlines, revealing the emotional toll of a generation disconnected from its heritage.

The narrative continues with global perspectives in Chapter 11, showing how countries like France and Japan balance handwriting with technology, offering models for America. Chapter 12 makes a compelling case for reviving cursive, emphasizing its historical, cognitive, and cultural value. Chapter 13 envisions cursive in the digital age, where tablets and apps can make it engaging for tech-savvy students. Finally, Chapter 14 imagines a new era for cursive, where schools, communities, and policymakers unite to restore this skill, ensuring that the Constitution and countless personal stories remain accessible. Together, these chapters tell a story of loss and possibility, a reminder that cursive is not just a skill but a key to our identity, a way to touch the past and shape the future.

The stakes are high. Without cursive, the Constitution risks becoming a museum piece, its words admired but unreadable. Family letters, diaries, and recipes, written in the flowing scripts of earlier generations, face the same fate, their stories locked in a language few can decipher. Yet the solution is within reach. By reintegrating cursive into education, leveraging digital tools, and fostering community engagement, we can revive this skill, ensuring that future generations can read the Constitution's parchment and hear their ancestors' voices. This book is a plea to act, to recognize cursive's value before it is lost forever. It is a call to pick up the pen, trace the loops of "We the People," and write a new chapter for a skill that has shaped our nation and can shape its future.

The journey begins in the classrooms of the past, where children bent over slates, their hands learning the rhythm of cursive as they copied the words of liberty. It continues in the archives, where millions of handwritten documents wait for readers who can unlock their secrets. It unfolds in the stories of families, teachers, and students, who feel the weight of a disconnected past and the hope of a revived future. Cursive is more than a script; it is a bridge, linking us to the Constitution, to our ancestors, to ourselves. As we navigate the digital age, we must decide whether to let this bridge crumble or to rebuild it, ensuring that the words of our past remain alive in the hands of our future. This book is an invitation to choose revival, to honor the legacy of cursive, and to keep the Constitution's promise readable for all.

Chapter 1: The Ancient Roots of Script

In the quiet shadows of history, where the dust of forgotten empires settles and the voices of the past whisper faintly, lies the story of humanity's greatest creation: writing. This is not a tale of battles or kings, but of symbols scratched into clay, carved on stone, and inked on fragile papyrus. These marks captured thoughts, preserved knowledge, and wove a thread through generations. Today, as keyboards replace pens and screens overshadow paper, we stand at a crossroads, risking the loss of a vital skill: cursive writing. Picture a future where the flowing, elegant script of the United States Constitution, penned by the hands of our Founding Fathers, becomes as unreadable as ancient glyphs. This chapter traces the origins of writing, from its earliest forms to the cursive scripts that paved the way for modern handwriting. By exploring these roots, we see why cursive is not just a relic but a bridge to our past, ensuring that foundational documents like the Constitution and countless personal records remain within our grasp.

The story begins long before cities rose or empires clashed. In the caves of prehistoric Europe, around 17,000 years ago, early humans painted vivid scenes of hunts and animals on walls, like those found in Lascaux, France. These images were not writing in the modern sense but the first steps toward it, visual stories that conveyed meaning without words. As societies grew more complex, around 8000 BCE in the Neolithic era, people in the Near East began using small clay tokens to track trade. Shaped like spheres, cones, or discs, these tokens represented sheep, grain, or oil. They were a simple system, born of necessity: as villages turned into towns and trade routes expanded, people needed ways to record and remember transactions. These tokens, stored in clay envelopes, were the seeds of a revolution.

By the late fourth millennium BCE, in the fertile lands between the Tigris and Euphrates rivers, known as Mesopotamia, this token system gave birth to something extraordinary: cuneiform. The name comes from the Latin word for wedge, reflecting the wedge-shaped marks made by pressing a reed stylus into soft clay. Around 3500 BCE, in the city of Uruk, the Sumerians, a people whose origins remain a mystery, developed what many consider the world's first true writing system. Their early tablets were practical, listing rations, temple goods, or labor records. Picture a clay tablet from 3100 BCE, its surface etched with signs tallying beer rations for workers. These marks were pictographs, simple drawings of objects: a head for a person, a star for the heavens. Writing, at this stage, was born not from poetry but from the mundane needs of trade and governance.

As Sumerian society grew, so did cuneiform. By 2500 BCE, the pictographs became more abstract, shaped by the medium of clay. The reed stylus, cut from river reeds, allowed for quick, angular strokes, turning curved drawings into wedge-like forms. This shift was transformative: writing began to capture sounds, not just objects. A sign for mouth could represent a syllable in other words, letting scribes record spoken language. This leap made cuneiform versatile, able to express laws, stories, and ideas. The Sumerians passed this gift to their neighbors, the Akkadians, who adapted it for their own language by 2300 BCE, creating bilingual texts that wove together cultures. Among the surviving tablets is the Epic of Gilgamesh, a tale of floods and heroes, etched in cuneiform, proving that writing could preserve not just records but the human spirit.

Cuneiform's relevance to our story lies in its efficiency. Writing on clay demanded speed. Scribes, often temple or palace officials, developed a streamlined style over centuries. By the Old

Babylonian period, around 2000 BCE, cuneiform signs were simpler, with fewer strokes, resembling a kind of early cursive. This adaptation let scribes jot down notes quickly, much like modern cursive connects letters for faster writing. Thousands of tablets, unearthed from cities like Nippur, show this evolution: early scripts used hundreds of signs, but later ones trimmed them down, prioritizing practicality over complexity.

Across the Mediterranean, another writing revolution unfolded in ancient Egypt around 3100 BCE. Hieroglyphs, meaning sacred carvings in Greek, appeared in the Nile Valley, used for everything from royal decrees to temple inscriptions. Unlike cuneiform's wedges, hieroglyphs were intricate, depicting birds, eyes, or reeds, often carved into stone or painted on tomb walls. But for daily tasks, like tax records or letters, Egyptian scribes turned to a faster script called hieratic. Written with ink on papyrus, hieratic was a cursive version of hieroglyphs, with simplified, flowing strokes. By 2000 BCE, it was the go-to script for priests and administrators, who could write swiftly on fragile sheets. Hieratic's cursive nature made it practical, much like the connected letters of modern handwriting, allowing thoughts to flow from mind to page with minimal interruption.

Hieratic gave way to an even more streamlined script by 1000 BCE: demotic. This cursive form was so simplified it barely resembled hieroglyphs, used for contracts, letters, and even literature. Demotic's rapid, connected strokes mirrored the needs of a bustling society, where speed mattered as much as clarity. The Rosetta Stone, carved in 196 BCE, bears demotic alongside hieroglyphs and Greek, a testament to its widespread use. Egypt's scripts show a pattern: as societies grew, so did the need for faster, more fluid writing, a trend that echoes in the cursive we know today.

Meanwhile, in the Levant, another milestone emerged around 1500 BCE: the alphabet. In the Sinai Peninsula, Semitic workers, possibly miners, developed a script called Proto-Sinaitic, inspired by Egyptian hieroglyphs but far simpler. Each sign stood for a sound, not a word or syllable, making it easier to learn and use. This proto-alphabet spread to the Phoenicians, a seafaring people, who refined it by 1100 BCE into a 22-letter system. The Phoenician alphabet, written in a flowing, semi-cursive style, was a game-changer. Merchants could jot down trade deals quickly, and the script's simplicity made it adaptable across languages. The Greeks adopted it by 800 BCE, adding vowels to create their alphabet, which in turn influenced the Romans.

The Roman alphabet, the ancestor of our own, brought cursive into sharper focus. By the first century CE, Roman scribes used a script called cursive capitals for everyday writing. Unlike the chiseled letters of stone inscriptions, cursive capitals were penned in ink on papyrus or wax tablets, with rounded, connected strokes for speed. Surviving fragments, like letters from Roman soldiers at Vindolanda in Britain, show this script in action: quick notes about supplies or personal matters, written in a flowing hand. By the fourth century CE, as Christianity spread, a new cursive script emerged, called New Roman Cursive, with even more fluid letter connections. This script, used for legal documents and early Christian texts, laid the groundwork for medieval scripts that would shape European handwriting.

In the early Middle Ages, as Rome's empire faded, monasteries became the guardians of writing. Monks in Europe developed scripts like the

Carolingian minuscule, a clear, lowercase style that emerged around 800 CE under Charlemagne's reforms. This script, with its rounded, connected letters, was designed for readability and speed, used to copy manuscripts of the Bible and classical texts. It was a direct ancestor of modern lowercase letters and cursive styles. Across the Irish Sea, Celtic monks crafted the Insular script, a flowing, ornate style used in masterpieces like the Book of Kells. These scripts, while distinct, shared a common thread: the need to balance beauty, clarity, and efficiency, much like the cursive that would later grace the US Constitution.

As we trace these ancient scripts, from cuneiform's wedges to Rome's flowing capitals, a pattern emerges: cursive forms arose from necessity. Scribes, merchants, and priests needed to write quickly, adapting their tools to the demands of clay, papyrus, or parchment. Each innovation built on the last, creating scripts that were not just functional but expressive, capturing the nuances of language and culture. Cursive, in its earliest forms, was not an art for the elite but a practical tool for the everyday, from tallying grain to penning prayers.

This ancient legacy matters because it connects directly to the cursive of our own history. The US Constitution, written in 1787, was penned in a copperplate script, a refined cursive style rooted in the traditions of European handwriting. Its elegant loops and flourishes were not mere decoration but a nod to centuries of scribal practice, where connected letters allowed thoughts to flow freely. Yet today, as cursive fades from classrooms, we risk losing more than a skill. We risk losing access to the documents that define us, from the Constitution to family letters tucked away in attics. If future generations cannot read the flowing script of 1787, the words of liberty and justice may become as distant as cuneiform, locked in a language no one can decipher.

The ancient roots of script remind us that writing is more than communication; it is a bridge across time. From Sumerian scribes pressing reeds into clay to monks illuminating manuscripts, each generation adapted writing to its needs, creating cursive forms that balanced speed and clarity. As we stand in the digital age, where typing overshadows handwriting, we must ask: what do we lose when we abandon cursive? The answer lies not just in the past but in the future, where the inability to read our own history could sever us from the documents and stories that shape who we are. This chapter is not just a history lesson but a call to remember: cursive is not obsolete, but a living link to the human story, one we cannot afford to break.

Chapter 2: Cursive in the Age of Enlightenment

As the sun rose over the Renaissance, casting its light on a Europe awakening from the slumber of the Middle Ages, a new era of ideas, art, and discovery began to flourish. The written word, once confined to the cloisters of monasteries, spilled into bustling cities, universities, and courts, carried by the hands of scholars, merchants, and scribes. Among the many revolutions of this period, from the printing press to the rediscovery of classical texts, was the refinement of cursive handwriting, a skill that would shape the way knowledge was recorded and shared. This chapter explores the pivotal role of cursive during the Renaissance and Enlightenment, tracing its evolution from medieval scripts to the elegant, flowing styles that defined early modern Europe and crossed the Atlantic to shape the documents of a new nation. The cursive script of this era, particularly the copperplate style, became the foundation for the handwriting of the United States Constitution, a testament to its enduring importance. To lose cursive today is to risk losing the ability to read the very documents that define our freedoms, a threat rooted in the neglect of a skill born in this transformative age.

The Renaissance, spanning roughly from the 14th to the 17th centuries, was a time of rebirth, a rediscovery of ancient Greek and Roman knowledge that sparked advances in art, science, and literature. Writing, too, underwent a transformation. In the Middle Ages, monks had preserved texts in scripts like the Carolingian minuscule, a clear, lowercase style developed around 800 CE under Charlemagne. This script, with its rounded letters and careful spacing, was designed for readability, used to copy sacred and classical texts. But as the Renaissance dawned, the demand for writing grew beyond the monastery. Merchants needed records for trade, scholars penned treatises, and nobles exchanged letters across expanding empires. The slow, deliberate scripts of the past were too cumbersome for this dynamic world. Enter cursive, a term derived from the Latin *cursus*, meaning running, which described scripts where letters flowed together, allowing scribes to write with speed and grace.

One of the earliest Renaissance cursive scripts was the *chancery hand*, born in the Italian city-states of the 14th century. Florence, Venice, and Rome were hubs of commerce and culture, where bureaucrats and secretaries needed a fast, legible script for official documents. The chancery hand, also called *cancelleresca*, was developed in the papal chancery, the administrative heart of the Catholic Church. Unlike the angular Gothic scripts of northern Europe, which were dense and ornate, chancery hand was light and fluid, with rounded letters and connected strokes. Its creator, Niccolò Niccoli, a Florentine scholar and book collector, sought a script that was both beautiful and practical. By 1400, his chancery hand was used for papal bulls, diplomatic letters, and legal records, its elegance reflecting the humanist ideals of clarity and harmony. Scribes trained in this script could produce documents quickly, their pens gliding across parchment with a rhythm that echoed the era's intellectual vitality.

The chancery hand's influence spread rapidly, thanks to the invention of the printing press around 1450 by Johannes Gutenberg. While printing revolutionized the spread of books, handwritten documents remained essential for personal and official communication. Printers, seeking to mimic the beauty of manuscripts, modeled their typefaces on cursive scripts like chancery hand. Aldus Manutius, a Venetian printer, introduced *italic* type in 1501, inspired directly by Niccoli's script. Italic, with its slanted, flowing letters, became a sensation, used in pocket-sized books that made literature accessible to a growing middle class. But italic was more than a typeface; it was a handwritten style taught to students and scribes, who used it for letters, poetry, and notes. Its connected letters allowed for faster writing than the blocky Roman capitals, making it a favorite among scholars like Erasmus, who penned thousands of letters in a cursive hand to correspond with thinkers across Europe.

As the Renaissance gave way to the Enlightenment in the late 17th and 18th centuries, cursive evolved further, reflecting the era's emphasis on reason, order, and elegance. The Enlightenment, often called the Age of Reason, saw the rise of scientific inquiry, political philosophy, and global exploration. Writing became a tool not just for recording but for shaping ideas that would change the world. In England, a new cursive style emerged: *roundhand*, also known as copperplate. This script, named for the copper plates used to engrave handwriting manuals, was the pinnacle of cursive's development in Europe. Developed in the mid-17th century by writing masters like John Ayres and George Bickham, roundhand was characterized by its smooth, flowing lines, consistent letter shapes, and decorative flourishes. Unlike the chancery hand's simplicity, roundhand was ornate, with thick downstrokes and thin upstrokes that gave it a rhythmic, almost musical quality.

Copperplate was more than a script; it was a cultural phenomenon. Writing masters, who taught handwriting to the gentry and aspiring middle classes, published manuals like Bickham's *The Universal Penman* in 1743, a lavish collection of engraved scripts that showcased roundhand's versatility. These manuals were not just instructional but aspirational, teaching students to write with elegance and precision. Merchants used copperplate for ledgers, diplomats for treaties, and poets for manuscripts. Its clarity and beauty made it ideal for official documents, where legibility was as important as prestige. By the 18th century, copperplate had crossed the Atlantic, becoming the preferred script of colonial America's educated elite. It was this style that would grace the parchment of the United States Constitution, its loops and flourishes embodying the ideals of a fledgling nation.

The spread of cursive during the Enlightenment was driven by education. Schools, particularly in England and France, emphasized penmanship as a mark of refinement. Boys and girls of the upper and middle classes learned cursive through rigorous practice, copying model scripts from writing manuals. In France, the *écriture bâtarde*, a cursive script derived from chancery hand, was taught alongside roundhand, blending practicality with flair. These lessons were not just about writing but about discipline and social mobility. A fine hand could open doors, signaling education and status. For women, who were increasingly literate, cursive was a means of expression, used in diaries, letters, and household accounts. The act of writing in cursive, with its flowing strokes, became a ritual, connecting the writer to a broader world of ideas and culture.

Across the Atlantic, the colonies embraced cursive with equal fervor. In the 17th and 18th centuries, American schools, often one-room affairs, taught handwriting alongside reading and arithmetic. Writing masters, many trained in England, brought copperplate to Boston, Philadelphia, and Williamsburg. Colonial scribes used it for legal documents, land deeds, and correspondence, creating a written record of a growing society. The Virginia Gazette, one of the colonies' first newspapers, advertised writing manuals and penmanship lessons, reflecting cursive's importance. By the time of the American Revolution, copperplate was the script of choice for official documents, its elegance lending authority to the words of rebellion and governance.

The significance of cursive in this era cannot be overstated. It was the medium through which the Enlightenment's ideas were shared. Philosophers like John Locke and Jean-Jacques Rousseau wrote in cursive, their manuscripts filled with arguments about liberty and human rights. Scientists like Isaac Newton used it to jot down calculations and theories. In America, figures like Benjamin Franklin and Thomas Jefferson penned letters and drafts in flowing scripts, their handwriting a reflection of their disciplined minds. The Declaration of Independence, drafted in 1776, and the Constitution, finalized in 1787, were written in copperplate, their words preserved in a script that was both functional and symbolic. The Constitution's preamble, with its soaring call for a more perfect union, owes part of its power to the visual harmony of its handwritten form, a testament to cursive's ability to elevate words into art.

Yet cursive was not just for the elite. Ordinary people, from shopkeepers to farmers, used it in their daily lives. Letters between families separated by oceans, journals of settlers moving west, and recipes passed down through generations were all written in cursive. These documents, often tucked away in attics or archives, are the threads of our collective history. They tell stories of love, struggle, and hope, written in the same flowing script as the nation's founding documents. To lose the ability to read cursive is to lose these stories, to sever the connection between past and present. A young person today, unable to decipher a grandparent's letter or a historical deed, is cut off from a heritage that cursive once preserved.

The Enlightenment's cursive scripts were also a technological marvel, adapted to the tools of the time. Quill pens, made from goose or swan feathers, were the primary writing instruments. Scribes cut the quill's tip to create a nib, which they dipped in ink made from soot or plant extracts. The quill's flexibility allowed for the thick and thin strokes of copperplate, giving it a dynamic quality that modern pens struggle to replicate. Parchment and paper, though expensive, were widely used, their smooth surfaces ideal for cursive's flowing lines. Writing desks, portable inkstands, and sand shakers for drying ink were common tools, reflecting the care and ritual of handwriting. This technology, simple yet precise, made cursive accessible to anyone with patience and practice.

As the Enlightenment gave way to the modern era, cursive remained a cornerstone of communication. But the seeds of its decline were already sown. The invention of the typewriter in the 19th century and the rise of mass education shifted priorities, setting the stage for debates about handwriting's relevance. Yet in the 18th century, cursive was king, a symbol of progress and civilization. Its importance lay not just in its practicality but in its ability to capture the human hand's movement, a physical trace of thought and intention. The Constitution, with its copperplate script, is a monument to this era, its words a promise written in a hand that demanded skill and care.

Today, as cursive fades from classrooms, we risk losing more than a skill. We risk losing the ability to read the Constitution in its original form, to feel the weight of its words through the strokes of a quill. The Enlightenment taught us that knowledge is power, and cursive was the tool that spread that knowledge. From the chancery hand of Renaissance Italy to the copperplate of colonial America, cursive has been a bridge between minds and eras. To abandon it is to break that bridge, leaving future generations stranded, unable to read the documents that define their rights or the letters that tell their family's stories. This chapter is a reminder that cursive is not just a relic of the Enlightenment but a living link to our past, one we must preserve to keep our history alive.

Chapter 3: The Founding Fathers' Flourish

In the sweltering summer of 1787, in a modest Philadelphia hall, a group of men gathered to forge a new nation. Their debates echoed with ideas of liberty, governance, and unity, but their most enduring legacy was not just the words they spoke but the way they recorded them: in the flowing, elegant cursive of the United States Constitution. This document, penned in the copperplate script that defined the era, was more than a legal framework; it was a testament to the power of handwriting to capture the aspirations of a people. The cursive strokes of quills, wielded by figures like James Madison and Gouverneur Morris, carried the weight of revolution and the promise of a republic. This chapter delves into the pivotal role of cursive during the founding of the United States, exploring how it shaped the creation of the Constitution and other key documents, from the Declaration of Independence to personal letters that reveal the human side of the Founders. To lose cursive today is to risk losing the ability to read these foundational texts in their original form, severing a vital connection to the ideals that built a nation.

The late 18th century was a time of upheaval and possibility. The American colonies, newly freed from British rule, faced the daunting task of creating a government that balanced power and freedom. The men who gathered at the Constitutional Convention, known as the Founding Fathers, were a diverse group: lawyers, farmers, merchants, and scholars, united by a vision of self-governance. Among them were Thomas Jefferson, whose pen drafted the Declaration of Independence; James Madison, the architect of the Constitution's structure; and Gouverneur Morris, whose elegant prose gave the document its final form. Their tools were simple: quill pens, ink, and parchment. Their medium was cursive, a script inherited from Europe's Enlightenment but adapted to the needs of a new world. This flowing handwriting, with its loops and flourishes, was not just practical but symbolic, embodying the grace and precision of their revolutionary ideas.

Cursive in colonial America was rooted in the copperplate style, a refined script that had crossed the Atlantic from England. Popularized by writing masters like George Bickham, copperplate was characterized by its smooth, connected letters, thick downstrokes, and delicate upstrokes. It required skill and discipline, qualities prized by the educated elite who shaped the colonies' future. Writing masters taught it in schools and private lessons, using manuals filled with engraved examples of perfect script. In cities like Philadelphia and Boston, young men and women practiced cursive to prepare for careers in law, trade, or governance. For the Founders, cursive was more than a skill; it was a mark of civility, a way to signal their place in a society striving for order and legitimacy.

The Declaration of Independence, adopted on July 4, 1776, was the first major document to showcase cursive's role in the American experiment. Drafted primarily by Thomas Jefferson, the document was initially written in his own hand, a neat copperplate script that reflected his meticulous nature. Jefferson, a Virginia planter and lawyer, was known for his elegant handwriting, honed through years of study and correspondence. His draft, debated and revised by the Continental Congress, was then copied by a professional scribe, Timothy Matlack, whose bold cursive gave the final parchment its iconic look. Matlack's hand, with its large, confident loops and flourishes, made the Declaration a visual masterpiece, its script as powerful as its words. The famous signature of John Hancock, oversized and ornate, became a symbol of defiance, a cursive flourish that dared the British Crown to challenge American resolve.

The Constitution, written 11 years later, built on this tradition. The Constitutional Convention, held in Philadelphia's Independence Hall from May to September 1787, was a grueling affair. Delegates debated everything from representation to slavery, seeking a balance between state and federal power. James Madison, often called the Father of the Constitution, kept detailed notes in cursive, his small, precise script capturing the arguments that shaped the final document. These notes, later published as the *Debates in the Federal Convention*, are a window into the Founders' minds, written in the same flowing hand that defined their era. When the debates concluded, Gouverneur Morris, a delegate from Pennsylvania, was tasked with writing the final draft. Morris, known for his eloquence, crafted the Constitution's preamble and articles in a clear, elegant copperplate, ensuring every word was legible and authoritative.

The physical act of writing the Constitution was no small feat. Scribes used quill pens, cut from goose feathers, dipped in ink made from oak galls or soot. Parchment, made from animal skin, was the medium of choice for official documents, its smooth surface ideal for cursive's flowing lines. The Constitution's engrossed parchment, now preserved in the National Archives, measures 29 by 24 inches, its text meticulously arranged in two columns. The script, attributed to Jacob Shallus, a clerk for the Pennsylvania legislature, is a masterwork of copperplate, with consistent letter forms and careful spacing. Each delegate's signature, from George Washington's bold flourish to Roger Sherman's compact scrawl, reflects the individuality of cursive, a personal mark on a collective vision.

Cursive was not just for official documents; it was the lifeblood of communication in the founding era. The Founders were prolific letter writers, using cursive to share ideas, negotiate alliances, and build a nation. Benjamin Franklin, a printer and diplomat, wrote thousands of letters in a clear, rounded script, discussing everything from electricity to foreign policy. His correspondence with European thinkers, written in cursive, helped secure French support for the Revolution. John Adams and his wife, Abigail, exchanged hundreds of letters, their cursive hands revealing both political strategy and personal affection. Abigail's elegant script, taught to her as a young woman, carried her sharp intellect, urging her husband to "remember the ladies" in the new government. These letters, preserved in archives, are a treasure trove of history, but their cursive script is becoming unreadable to a generation taught only to type.

Beyond the Founders, cursive was a democratic skill, used by ordinary Americans to navigate a changing world. Merchants kept ledgers in flowing script, recording trade with Europe and the Caribbean. Farmers jotted down crop yields and debts in pocket notebooks, their cursive often rough but functional. Women, increasingly literate, used cursive for diaries, recipes, and letters, preserving family histories that might otherwise be lost. In rural towns, town clerks recorded births, marriages, and deaths in cursive, creating public records that remain vital for genealogists today. These documents, from land deeds to wills, were written in the same copperplate style as the Constitution, linking the personal to the political in a shared script.

The importance of cursive in this era went beyond practicality; it was a cultural symbol. A fine hand was a mark of education and refinement, a way to stand out in a society where literacy was not universal. For the Founders, cursive was a tool of persuasion, used to draft pamphlets, broadsides, and newspaper essays that rallied support for independence. The *Federalist Papers*, written by Alexander Hamilton, James Madison, and John Jay to promote the Constitution's ratification, were first drafted in cursive before being printed. The handwritten drafts, filled with corrections and marginal notes, show the Founders wrestling with ideas in real time, their cursive strokes capturing the urgency of the moment.

Cursive also played a role in the legal system of the new nation. Courts relied on handwritten records, from indictments to verdicts, all penned in copperplate. Lawyers like John Adams and Aaron Burr drafted briefs in cursive, their scripts reflecting their professional training. The Bill of Rights, added to the Constitution in 1791, was written in the same flowing hand, its amendments protecting freedoms of speech, religion, and assembly. These documents, now revered as the cornerstone of American law, were products of a cursive culture, where the act of writing was inseparable from the act of governing.

The education system of the founding era reinforced cursive's centrality. Schools, whether in bustling cities or rural villages, taught penmanship as a core skill. Children practiced on slates or paper, copying model scripts from writing manuals imported from England or printed in America. Teachers, often young men training for the clergy or law, drilled students in forming letters with precision. The goal was not just legibility but elegance, a reflection of the Enlightenment ideals that shaped the Founders' worldview. For enslaved Americans, who were often denied formal education, cursive was a rare and precious skill. Figures like Phillis Wheatley, a poet who learned to write in her teens, used cursive to compose verses that challenged the hypocrisy of slavery, her script a quiet act of rebellion.

The physical tools of cursive shaped its character. Quill pens required constant sharpening, a task that demanded patience and skill. Ink, prone to smudging, had to be carefully applied, with sand sprinkled to dry it. Paper, though more common than in earlier centuries, was still a luxury, often reused or cut into small sheets for letters. Writing desks, with their slanted surfaces and inkwells, were fixtures in homes and offices, symbols of the importance of handwriting. The Founders, many of whom traveled frequently, carried portable writing kits, allowing them to pen letters or drafts on the move. These tools, combined with the discipline of cursive, made writing a deliberate act, one that connected the writer to their words in a way typing cannot replicate.

The cursive of the founding era was not without flaws. Variations in handwriting could lead to misreadings, especially in legal documents where a single letter could change a contract's meaning. The lack of standardization meant that scripts varied widely, from Jefferson's neat hand to Washington's more angular style. Yet these imperfections were part of cursive's charm, reflecting the individuality of each writer. The Constitution's engrossed parchment, with its occasional ink blots and corrections, is a reminder that even the most important documents were human creations, shaped by the fallible hands of their authors.

As the United States grew, cursive remained a cornerstone of communication. The 19th century saw the rise of standardized scripts like the Spencerian method, but the copperplate of the founding era left an indelible mark. It was the script of revolution, of nation-building, and of personal connection. Today, as cursive fades from school curricula, we face a future where the Constitution's original parchment may be unreadable to most Americans. The signatures of Washington, Franklin, and Madison, once symbols of unity and resolve, risk becoming mere decorations, their meaning lost to a generation unfamiliar with their script.

The Founding Fathers' flourish was more than a style; it was a statement. Their cursive captured the urgency of their ideas, the weight of their decisions, and the hope of their vision. To preserve that vision, we must preserve the ability to read it. The Constitution, with its elegant script, is not just a document but a living link to the past, a reminder of the sacrifices and dreams that built a nation. If we lose cursive, we lose more than a skill; we lose the ability to touch the words that shaped our freedoms, to see the Founders' hands at work in the strokes of their quills. This chapter is a call to remember that cursive is not a relic but a key to our history, one we must keep alive to honor the legacy of those who wrote it.

Chapter 4: Cursive as a Pillar of Education

In the bustling classrooms of 19th-century America, where the hum of recitation and the scratch of quills filled the air, cursive handwriting stood as a cornerstone of learning. It was more than a skill; it was a rite of passage, a discipline that shaped young minds and connected them to the nation's founding documents. From one-room schoolhouses in rural New England to urban academies in growing cities, children bent over slates and paper, tracing the elegant loops and flourishes of copperplate script. This practice was not merely about forming letters but about forging a link to the past, ensuring that texts like the United States Constitution, written in flowing cursive, remained accessible to future generations. As cursive fades from modern curricula, we risk losing this connection, leaving the words of liberty and justice locked in a script few can read. This chapter explores how cursive became a pillar of education in early America, its role in shaping literacy and citizenship, and why its decline threatens our ability to engage with historical records, from the Constitution to family letters.

The roots of cursive's prominence in American education trace back to the colonial era, when literacy was a privilege, not a right. In the 17th and 18th centuries, education was often informal, provided by parents, tutors, or small dame schools run by women in their homes. Reading was taught first, often using the Bible or hornbooks, but writing came later, reserved for those destined for commerce, law, or governance. Cursive, particularly the copperplate style brought from England, was the script of choice, valued for its speed and elegance. By the time of the American Revolution, schools began to formalize, and cursive became a standard part of the curriculum, especially for boys training for professional roles. Girls, too, learned cursive, using it to write letters or keep household records, a skill that marked them as educated and refined.

The early 19th century marked a turning point for American education. The common school movement, led by reformers like Horace Mann, sought to make education universal, free, and standardized. By the 1830s, public schools were spreading across the young nation, from Massachusetts to the expanding frontier. These schools, often simple log buildings with a single teacher, emphasized the "three Rs": reading, writing, and arithmetic. Writing, in this context, meant cursive handwriting, seen as essential for communication and civic life. The Constitution,

Declaration of Independence, and other founding documents were written in cursive, and students were expected to read and copy these texts as part of their education. Teachers used writing manuals, imported from England or printed in America, to guide lessons, with copperplate as the gold standard.

One of the most influential figures in this era was Platt Rogers Spencer, a teacher and penman from Ohio who revolutionized handwriting education. In the 1840s, Spencer developed the Spencerian script, a simplified version of copperplate that was easier to learn yet retained its elegance. With its flowing, semi-connected letters and graceful flourishes, Spencerian became the dominant cursive style in American schools. Spencer believed that handwriting was a moral and intellectual discipline, akin to music or art. His *Spencerian Penmanship* manuals, first published in 1848, included detailed instructions and practice sheets, with students copying phrases like "Knowledge is power" or passages from the Constitution. These exercises were not just about penmanship but about instilling values of diligence and precision, qualities deemed essential for a democratic society.

The Spencerian system spread rapidly, adopted by schools, businesses, and government offices. Its popularity stemmed from its balance of beauty and practicality. Unlike the ornate copperplate of the 18th century, Spencerian was designed for everyday use, with smoother transitions between letters that allowed for faster writing. Students spent hours practicing, dipping quill pens or early steel nibs into inkwells, their hands moving in rhythmic patterns to form perfect ovals and slants. The goal was not just legibility but mastery, a skill that set one apart in a society where handwritten documents were the backbone of communication. Clerks, lawyers, and merchants relied on Spencerian for ledgers, contracts, and correspondence, while ordinary citizens used it for letters, diaries, and family records.

Cursive's role in education extended beyond technical skill. It was a gateway to literacy, helping students internalize the structure of language. By forming letters in a connected flow, students learned to see words as cohesive units, improving their reading and spelling. Teachers often had students copy passages from historical texts, including the Constitution or Lincoln's speeches, reinforcing civic lessons through the act of writing.

For many, this was their first encounter with the nation's founding ideals, written in the same script as the originals. A child copying "We the People" in cursive was not just practicing penmanship but engaging with the principles of democracy, a tactile connection to the nation's foundation.

The classroom environment of the 19th century was rigorous, even austere. Students sat at wooden desks, often shared, with inkwells embedded in the surface. Teachers, frequently young women barely older than their pupils, enforced strict discipline, correcting posture and grip to ensure proper letter formation. Writing lessons began with basic strokes lines, curves, and loops before progressing to individual letters and words. Copybooks, filled with model scripts, were prized possessions, their pages worn from repeated use. Mistakes were costly; paper was expensive, and ink smudges could ruin a lesson. Yet this rigor produced results: by the end of elementary school, most students could write a legible cursive hand, a skill they carried into adulthood.

Cursive was especially important for marginalized groups, for whom literacy was a path to empowerment. In the post-Civil War era, freed

African Americans flocked to schools established by the Freedmen's Bureau, eager to learn reading and writing. Cursive, taught alongside print, was a symbol of freedom, a way to claim agency in a society that had long denied it. Teachers like Charlotte Forten, a Black educator in South Carolina, used Spencerian manuals to teach former slaves, who practiced writing their names in cursive as a declaration of identity. For women, cursive was equally significant. As more girls attended school, they used handwriting to express themselves in letters, journals, and poetry, their cursive scripts often more refined than those of their male peers.

The tools of cursive education were simple but demanding. Quill pens, still common in the early 19th century, gave way to steel nibs by the 1850s, which were more durable and precise. Ink, made from iron gall or plant dyes, was prone to clotting, requiring careful handling. Paper, though more affordable than in colonial times, was still a precious resource, often reused or cut into small sheets for practice. Writing desks, with their slanted surfaces, were designed for cursive, allowing the hand to move fluidly across the page. Teachers used rulers or pointers to guide students' hands, ensuring the 52-degree slant recommended by Spencerian manuals. These tools, combined with hours of practice, made cursive a craft, one that required patience and skill.

Cursive's prominence in education was not without challenges. Rural schools often lacked resources, with students sharing slates or writing on scraps of paper. Teachers, underpaid and overworked, struggled to teach large classes, sometimes neglecting handwriting for more pressing subjects. Handwriting quality varied widely; a merchant's elegant script might contrast with a farmer's rough scrawl. Yet even these variations underscored cursive's universality. Whether polished or crude, it was the common language of written communication, used in everything from legal deeds to love letters. The Constitution, with its copperplate script, was a model for students, who copied its preamble or amendments as exercises, embedding its words in their minds and hands.

By the late 19th century, cursive faced new pressures. The invention of the typewriter, patented in 1868, began to shift how documents were produced, especially in businesses and government. Yet cursive remained dominant in schools, seen as essential for personal and professional life. The

Palmer Method, introduced in the 1880s by Austin Palmer, built on Spencerian's legacy, emphasizing arm movements over finger motions to reduce fatigue. Palmer's manuals, with their repetitive drills, became a staple in classrooms, training students to write quickly and legibly. This method, used well into the 20th century, produced generations of Americans who could read and write cursive with ease, ensuring that historical documents remained accessible.

Cursive's role in education also had a cultural dimension. It was a mark of refinement, a skill that distinguished the educated from the unlettered. In an era when many Americans were immigrants or first-generation citizens, cursive was a way to assimilate, to claim a place in the nation's story. Schools taught it as a civic duty, preparing students to engage with the documents that defined their rights. A young person who could read the Constitution in its original script felt a connection to the Founders, their cursive hand a bridge to 1787. This connection was not abstract but tangible, rooted in the physical act of writing.

The decline of cursive in modern education threatens this legacy. When the Common Core

Standards, adopted in 2010, removed cursive from mandatory curricula, they prioritized typing over handwriting, reflecting a belief that digital skills were more relevant. Yet this shift overlooks the cognitive and cultural benefits of cursive. Studies show that handwriting improves memory, fine motor skills, and reading comprehension, benefits that typing cannot replicate. More critically, without cursive, students cannot read the original Constitution, Declaration of Independence, or countless personal records, from grandparents' letters to old deeds. These documents, written in the flowing scripts of the 19th century, are at risk of becoming relics, their meaning lost to a generation trained only in print or pixels.

The 19th-century classroom, with its inkwells and copybooks, was a crucible for cursive's enduring legacy. It was where children learned not just to write but to think, to connect with the ideas and stories that shaped their world. The Constitution, with its elegant copperplate, was a constant presence, its words copied by countless hands as a lesson in both penmanship and patriotism. To abandon cursive is to break this chain, to leave future generations unable to read the documents that define their freedoms or the letters that tell their family's stories. This chapter is a reminder that cursive was not just a pillar of education but a foundation of citizenship, a skill that must be preserved to keep our history alive and accessible.

Chapter 5: The Golden Era of Handwritten Communication

In the vibrant tapestry of 19th and early 20th century America, cursive handwriting wove a thread that connected hearts, minds, and institutions. It was the golden era of handwritten communication, a time when the flowing strokes of a pen carried the weight of personal bonds, professional agreements, and national identity. From love letters sent across oceans to legal deeds securing land, cursive was the lifeblood of a society that valued the written word as a tangible extension of human experience. The United States Constitution, penned in elegant copperplate, stood as a beacon of this era, its cursive script embodying the ideals of a young nation. Yet, as cursive fades from modern education, we risk losing the ability to read not only the Constitution but also the countless personal and historical documents that define our past. This chapter explores the zenith of cursive's role in American life, illustrating its ubiquity in everyday communication and its critical importance in preserving our heritage, from official records to intimate letters tucked away in family archives.

The 19th century was a time of expansion and transformation in the United States. The nation stretched westward, railroads crisscrossed the continent, and cities swelled with immigrants seeking opportunity. Amid this growth, cursive handwriting was the universal language of written communication. Unlike today's digital messages, which vanish into the ether of deleted files, handwritten documents were physical artifacts, cherished for their permanence and personal touch. Every letter, diary entry, and contract bore the unique mark of its writer's hand, a cursive script that reflected personality, education, and intent. Whether in the neat Spencerian loops of a schoolteacher or the hurried scrawl of a frontiersman, cursive was the medium through which Americans recorded their lives and shaped their society.

At the heart of this era was the letter, a cornerstone of personal and professional life. Families separated by migration or war relied on cursive letters to maintain bonds. During the Civil War, soldiers on both sides penned letters to loved ones, their words written in flowing script on thin paper, often folded into small envelopes and carried hundreds of miles. A Union soldier in Virginia might write to his wife in Ohio, describing camp life in a cramped, cursive hand, his ink smudged by rain or sweat. These letters, preserved in archives or family collections, are windows into the past, revealing the fears, hopes, and resilience of ordinary people. A Confederate nurse, writing to her brother, might use the same Spencerian script taught in schools, her cursive loops a testament to her education despite the chaos of war. These documents, written in the same style as the Constitution, are now at risk of becoming unreadable, their stories lost if cursive is forgotten.

Beyond personal correspondence, cursive was essential in professional spheres. Merchants kept ledgers in flowing script, recording sales of cotton, lumber, or whiskey in precise columns. A New York shopkeeper in 1850 might spend evenings updating his books, his cursive hand ensuring clarity for future audits. Lawyers drafted contracts, wills, and deeds in cursive, their scripts lending authority to legal agreements. A land deed from the Oklahoma Territory, written in elegant Spencerian, might secure a family's claim to a homestead, its cursive text a binding promise in a new frontier. These documents, like the Constitution, were meant to endure, their legibility crucial for future generations to understand property rights or family histories.

Cursive's role in government was equally vital. Town clerks across the nation recorded births, marriages, and deaths in cursive, creating public records that remain essential for genealogists and historians. A Vermont clerk in 1870 might spend hours entering vital statistics in a ledger, her neat script ensuring accuracy for decades to come. Court records, from indictments to verdicts, were penned in cursive, as were legislative journals and official correspondence. The Constitution itself, copied by hand for distribution to states, was a model for these records, its copperplate script a standard of clarity and prestige. These government documents, preserved in archives, are a direct link to the nation's founding, but their cursive text is inaccessible to those who cannot read it.

The ubiquity of cursive was no accident; it was rooted in the education system described in the previous chapter. By the mid-19th century, the Spencerian script, with its flowing, semi-connected letters, dominated American schools. Children learned cursive through rigorous practice, copying moral maxims or passages from historical texts. Teachers emphasized posture, pen grip, and letter formation, drilling students in the art of smooth, legible writing. This training produced a generation of Americans fluent in cursive, capable of reading and writing everything from the Constitution to personal journals. The act of copying the Constitution's preamble, with its call for a "more perfect Union," was both a penmanship exercise and a lesson in civic duty, embedding the nation's ideals in young minds.

Cursive's versatility made it ideal for a society on the move. The 19th century saw waves of migration, from Irish immigrants fleeing famine to pioneers heading west for gold or land. Letters were lifelines, connecting those who left with those who stayed behind. An Irish woman in Boston might write to her family in Cork, her cursive script carrying news of factory work or a new child. A settler in Oregon, writing to relatives in Virginia, might describe the hardships of the trail in a hurried but legible hand. These letters, often stored in trunks or attics, are treasures of family history, but their cursive text is becoming a mystery to descendants unfamiliar with the script. Without cursive literacy, a great-grandchild might hold a letter from 1860 and see only indecipherable loops, its story locked away.

Women, in particular, found cursive a powerful tool of expression. As literacy rates rose, more women wrote diaries, letters, and recipes, their cursive hands capturing the texture of daily life. A farmwife in Iowa might record her day in a journal, her Spencerian script detailing chores, harvests, or a child's illness. These diaries, often passed down through generations, are intimate portraits of resilience and community, written in the same flowing style as official documents. Recipes, scribbled in cursive on scraps of paper, preserved family traditions, from cornbread to apple pie. These personal documents, like the Constitution, rely on cursive for their accessibility, a reminder that history is not just in grand texts but in the small, handwritten moments of everyday life.

The tools of cursive communication were simple yet evocative. Quill pens, used early in the century, gave way to steel nibs, which offered precision without constant sharpening. Ink, made from iron gall or plant extracts, was stored in glass inkwells, often embedded in school desks or carried in portable cases. Paper, though more affordable than in colonial times, was still valued, with writers using both sides or cutting sheets into smaller pieces for letters. Writing desks, with their slanted surfaces and compartments for pens and ink, were common in homes, symbolizing the importance of handwriting. Sand, sprinkled to dry wet ink, added a tactile ritual to the act of writing, its grains swept away to reveal crisp, flowing script.

Cursive's aesthetic appeal was part of its power. The Spencerian script, with its graceful curves and flourishes, was seen as an art form, a reflection of the writer's character. A well-crafted letter, with consistent letter heights and elegant loops, signaled education and refinement. Businesses capitalized on this, employing clerks with fine hands to impress clients or partners. A bank in Philadelphia might display ledgers in pristine cursive, their neatness a sign of trustworthiness. Wedding invitations, calling cards, and even advertisements were often handwritten or engraved to mimic cursive, their beauty enhancing their message. This attention to form made cursive a cultural ideal, one shared by the Constitution's elegant script.

The Civil War, from 1861 to 1865, was a high point for cursive's role in communication. Letters between soldiers and families were a lifeline, carrying news of battles, injuries, or survival. Officers wrote orders in cursive, their hurried scripts reflecting the urgency of war. Abraham Lincoln's own hand, seen in drafts of the Emancipation Proclamation or the Gettysburg Address, was a clear, cursive scrawl, its simplicity contrasting with the weight of his words. These documents, like the Constitution, were products of a cursive culture, their handwritten forms a testament to the human effort behind them. Today, students who cannot read cursive may struggle to decipher Lincoln's drafts or a soldier's letter, losing a direct connection to this pivotal era.

Cursive also played a role in the nation's cultural life. Poets and writers, from Emily Dickinson to Walt Whitman, drafted their works in cursive, their scripts reflecting their creative process. Dickinson's poems, written in a tight, idiosyncratic hand, were often scrawled on envelopes or scraps, their cursive lines capturing her fleeting thoughts. Whitman's notebooks, filled with cursive jottings, show the evolution of *Leaves of Grass*, his script as expansive as his verse. These manuscripts, preserved in libraries, are not just literary artifacts but historical ones, their cursive text a link to the minds that shaped American culture. Without cursive literacy, these works become museum pieces, admired but not understood.

The late 19th and early 20th centuries saw cursive's influence persist, even as new technologies emerged. The typewriter, gaining popularity after

1870, began to replace handwritten documents in business, but cursive remained dominant in personal and educational contexts. The Palmer Method, introduced in the 1880s, refined Spencerian's principles, emphasizing arm movements for faster, less fatiguing writing. Schools adopted it widely, ensuring that cursive remained a core skill. Immigrants, eager to integrate, learned cursive as part of Americanization programs, their scripts a badge of belonging. By 1900, cursive was so ingrained that it was unthinkable for an educated person not to read or write it.

Yet the seeds of cursive's decline were sown in this era. The rise of typewriters, followed by telephones and telegraphs, began to shift communication away from handwriting. By the early 20th century, schools faced pressure to teach practical skills like typing, especially as offices modernized. Still, cursive held strong, seen as essential for reading historical documents and maintaining personal connections. The Constitution, with its copperplate script, remained a touchstone, its text copied in classrooms as a lesson in both penmanship and patriotism.

Today, the decline of cursive threatens this legacy. When schools dropped it from curricula, prioritizing keyboards over pens, they severed a link to the golden era of handwritten communication. Without cursive, the Constitution's original parchment, with its flowing script, becomes a relic, its words inaccessible to those who cannot read them. The same is true for countless personal documents: letters from soldiers, diaries of pioneers, recipes from grandmothers. These are not just artifacts but stories, written in the cursive that defined an era. To lose this skill is to lose a piece of our humanity, the ability to touch the past through the strokes of a pen.

This chapter celebrates the golden era of handwritten communication, when cursive was the heartbeat of American life. It was a time when every letter, ledger, and law was crafted by hand, in a script that mirrored the nation's aspirations. The Constitution, with its elegant copperplate, is a monument to this era, its words a call to preserve the skill that makes them readable. As we stand in a digital age, we must recognize that cursive is not just a relic but a key to our history, a way to keep the voices of the past alive in the hands of the future.

Chapter 6: The Digital Shift Begins

As the 19th century gave way to the 20th, the United States stood on the cusp of a technological revolution that would reshape communication. The quill pens and inkwells that had defined the golden era of cursive handwriting began to share space with new machines: typewriters, telegraphs, and eventually computers. These inventions promised speed and efficiency, but they also sparked a subtle shift away from the flowing cursive scripts that had recorded the nation's history, from the United States Constitution to personal letters. The post-World War II era, with its rapid industrialization and embrace of modernity, marked the beginning of a decline in cursive's dominance, as society prioritized mechanized communication over the art of handwriting. This chapter explores the early stages of this digital shift, focusing on how technological advancements, educational changes, and cultural attitudes began to erode cursive's centrality, setting the stage for a future where foundational documents like the Constitution might become unreadable to generations unfamiliar with their script. The story of this transition is not just about machines replacing pens, but about a society grappling with progress while risking the loss of a vital link to its past.

The seeds of the digital shift were sown in the late 19th century, when the typewriter emerged as a game-changer. Patented in 1868 by Christopher Latham Sholes, the typewriter offered a faster, more uniform alternative to handwriting. By the 1880s, businesses in cities like New York and Chicago began adopting typewriters for correspondence, invoices, and contracts. The machine's clacking keys produced crisp, printed text, free of the smudges and variations of cursive script. For offices overwhelmed with paperwork, this was a revelation. A clerk could type a letter in minutes, where writing it in cursive might take much longer. The Remington Typewriter Company, founded in 1873, marketed its machines as tools of progress, promising to streamline commerce and bureaucracy. By 1900, typewriters were common in banks, law firms, and government offices, their output replacing the elegant Spencerian or Palmer scripts that had once defined professional documents.

Yet the typewriter's rise did not immediately threaten cursive's place in everyday life. In the early 20th century, handwriting remained a core skill, taught rigorously in schools. The Palmer Method, with its emphasis on fluid, arm-driven cursive, dominated classrooms, ensuring that students could write letters, keep journals, and read historical texts like the Constitution. Personal communication still relied heavily on cursive. Families exchanged handwritten letters, soldiers sent notes from World War I trenches, and small-town clerks recorded vital records in flowing script. The typewriter was a tool for businesses, not homes, and its high cost kept it out of reach for many. Cursive, with its low barrier to entry a pen, ink, and paper was democratic, accessible to anyone with a basic education.

The real shift began after World War II, when technological and social changes accelerated. The war had spurred innovations in electronics, from radar to early computers, laying the groundwork for the digital age. In the 1950s, as America embraced a postwar economic boom, offices modernized rapidly. Typewriters became more affordable, with models like the IBM Selectric, introduced in 1961, offering features like interchangeable fonts and electric keys. Businesses trained armies of typists, often women, to handle the growing volume of paperwork. Government agencies, too, adopted typewriters for reports, memos, and forms, reducing reliance on handwritten records. The cursive ledgers and letters of the 19th century began to give way to typed documents, their uniformity prized in an era of efficiency.

Education, however, remained a stronghold for cursive, though cracks were beginning to show. Schools in the 1950s still taught handwriting as a core subject, with students practicing cursive drills on lined paper. Teachers used copybooks, descendants of the Spencerian and Palmer manuals, to guide students in forming perfect loops and slants. The Constitution, with its copperplate script, was a common text for copying, serving as both a penmanship exercise and a lesson in civics. Yet the postwar era brought new priorities. The launch of Sputnik by the Soviet Union in 1957 sparked a national panic about America's technological lag, leading to a push for science and math education. Schools faced pressure to prepare students for a modern workforce, where typing was becoming a valued skill. Typing classes, once rare, began appearing in high schools, with rows of students practicing on clunky machines. Cursive, while still taught, started to compete for time in crowded curricula.

The 1960s and 1970s saw this trend intensify. The rise of computers, though still in its infancy, hinted at a future where digital communication would dominate. Early computers, like the IBM 360 introduced in 1964, were used by businesses and universities for data processing, their output printed on dot-matrix printers. These machines, though far from personal, signaled a shift toward mechanized text. Meanwhile, the typewriter's ubiquity grew, with portable models entering homes and schools. Secretarial schools flourished, training young women to type at high speeds, their skills in demand in corporate America. Cursive, once the universal standard for written communication, began to feel outdated in professional settings, where typed documents were seen as cleaner and more modern.

Cultural attitudes also began to shift. The postwar generation, raised in an era of television, cars, and consumer culture, valued speed and convenience. Handwritten letters, while still common, faced competition from telephones, which offered instant communication. A family in California could call relatives in New York, bypassing the need for a cursive letter that took days to arrive. The postal service, once the backbone of handwritten communication, saw a rise in typed business mail, from bills to advertisements. Cursive remained a personal act, used for love letters, thank-you notes, and diaries, but its role in public life was shrinking. A 1970s office worker might still write a quick note in cursive, but formal correspondence was increasingly typed, its uniformity a symbol of professionalism.

In education, the debate over cursive's relevance began to emerge. In the 1970s, as schools grappled with overcrowded classrooms and budget constraints, some educators questioned the time spent on handwriting. Progressive education movements, emphasizing creativity and critical thinking, argued that rote drills like cursive practice were outdated. The rise of standardized testing, driven by federal policies like the Elementary and Secondary Education Act of 1965, shifted focus to measurable skills like reading and math. Typing, seen as a practical skill for the modern workforce, gained traction, with schools investing in typewriter labs. A 1975 survey of high school curricula found that typing classes were offered in nearly half of American schools, often at the expense of advanced handwriting instruction. Cursive was still taught, but its prominence was waning, relegated to early elementary grades.

This shift had implications for how Americans engaged with their history. The Constitution, Declaration of Independence, and other founding documents, all written in cursive, were still taught in schools, but students spent less time copying them by hand. Instead, textbooks printed these texts in modern fonts, making them easier to read but distancing students from the original scripts. A child in 1970 might learn about the Constitution's preamble but never see its copperplate parchment, let alone try to read it. This subtle disconnect marked the beginning of a generational gap, where the cursive of the past was becoming less familiar. Letters from grandparents, written in flowing script, might puzzle a teenager more comfortable with typed notes or early digital displays.

The rise of computers in the 1980s accelerated this trend. Personal computers, like the Apple II and IBM PC, brought digital text into homes and schools. Word processors, such as WordStar and later Microsoft Word, allowed users to type, edit, and print documents with ease. A college student in 1985 could write a term paper on a computer, print it in a clean font, and submit it without ever touching a pen. Businesses embraced computers for their speed and versatility, replacing typewriters with desktop systems. Government offices followed suit, digitizing records and reducing reliance on handwritten documents. The cursive ledgers and correspondence of the 19th century were being archived, replaced by printed forms and digital files.

Yet cursive held on in personal and educational contexts. In the 1980s, most elementary schools still taught cursive, often in third or fourth grade, as a rite of passage. Students practiced forming letters with pencils on wide-ruled paper, their teachers guiding them through loops and connections. The Palmer Method, though less common, was still used, alongside newer systems like D'Nealian, which aimed to bridge print and cursive with simpler forms. These lessons were seen as essential for developing fine motor skills and preparing students to read historical texts. A teacher might display a facsimile of the Constitution, pointing out its elegant script as a link to the nation's founding. Parents, too, valued cursive, encouraging children to write thank-you notes or keep journals in flowing script.

Despite its persistence, cursive faced growing challenges. The 1980s saw a surge in educational reforms, driven by reports like *A Nation at Risk* in

1983, which called for a focus on science, technology, and vocational skills. Schools invested in computer labs, teaching students to type and use basic software. By 1990, typing was a standard high school course, while cursive was often limited to a few weeks of instruction. The rise of email, pioneered by systems like ARPANET and later commercial services, further reduced the need for handwritten letters. A businessperson could send a typed email in seconds, where a cursive letter might take hours to write and days to deliver. The personal touch of cursive was still valued, but its practicality was fading in a world of instant communication.

The cultural shift was evident in everyday life. By the 1990s, typed documents dominated professional settings, from resumes to legal briefs. Handwritten notes were still common, but they were often in print, not cursive, as people found block letters faster to write and easier to read. The rise of ballpoint pens, which replaced fountain pens, also changed handwriting habits. Ballpoints required less pressure, encouraging simpler, less connected scripts. A 1990s office worker might jot a quick note in print, reserving cursive for personal tasks like signing checks or writing holiday cards. The Constitution's copperplate script, once a model for penmanship, was becoming a historical curiosity, admired in museums but rarely studied in classrooms.

This digital shift had profound implications for historical literacy. Archives across the country held millions of cursive documents: letters, diaries, deeds, and government records, all written in the scripts of the 19th and early 20th centuries. The Constitution, with its elegant parchment, was a prime example, its text a challenge for anyone untrained in cursive. A 1990s student, taught only print, might struggle to read a handwritten letter from the Civil War or a family Bible's inscriptions. Historians and genealogists, who relied on cursive records for research, began to notice a growing gap. Young volunteers in archives, accustomed to typed text, often needed training to decipher handwritten manuscripts, a skill their grandparents took for granted.

The decline of cursive was not deliberate but a byproduct of progress. Schools, under pressure to prepare students for a digital economy, prioritized typing and computer skills. Parents, eager for their children to succeed, supported this focus, seeing cursive as a relic of a slower era. Yet this shift overlooked cursive's deeper value. Beyond its practical use, cursive connected generations to their past, allowing them to read the words of the Founders, soldiers, and ancestors in their original form. A letter from a World War II soldier, written in cursive, carried not just words but the weight of his hand, a physical trace of his experience. The Constitution, with its flowing script, was a living document, meant to be read and understood by all Americans, not just scholars with specialized training.

As the 20th century closed, cursive remained a part of education, but its role was diminishing. The rise of the internet, with its emails, chat rooms, and digital documents, further marginalized handwriting. By 2000, many schools taught cursive only briefly, if at all, focusing instead on keyboarding skills. The stage was set for the 21st century, when the Common Core Standards would remove cursive from mandatory curricula, cementing its decline. Yet the documents of the past, from the Constitution to family letters, remained in cursive, waiting for readers who could unlock their meaning.

This chapter marks the beginning of a pivotal transition, when the tools of modernity began to overshadow the art of handwriting. The typewriter, computer, and telephone promised efficiency, but they came at a cost: the slow erosion of a skill that had defined communication for centuries. The Constitution, with its copperplate script, stands as a reminder of what we risk losing. To read its words in their original form is to touch the hands of the Founders, to feel the weight of their vision. If we abandon cursive, we abandon that connection, leaving our history to fade into unreadable lines. This is not just a story of technology but of choices, and the choice to preserve cursive is a choice to keep our past alive.

Chapter 7: Common Core and the Cursive Purge

In the early 21st century, a seismic shift in American education threatened to sever a vital link to the nation's past. The introduction of the Common Core State Standards in 2010, a sweeping initiative to standardize K-12 education across the United States, marked a turning point in the history of cursive handwriting. For centuries, cursive had been a cornerstone of learning, connecting students to foundational documents like the United States Constitution and personal records like family letters. Its flowing script, from the copperplate of the Founding Fathers to the Spencerian of the 19th century, was not just a means of communication but a bridge to history. Yet, with the stroke of a policy pen, Common Core removed cursive from mandatory curricula, prioritizing typing and digital literacy over the art of handwriting. This chapter explores the origins, rationale, and consequences of this decision, known as the cursive purge, and its profound implications for a future where the Constitution and countless historical documents may become unreadable to generations untrained in their script.

The Common Core Standards emerged from a desire to address perceived shortcomings in American education. By the early 2000s, concerns about global competitiveness, fueled by reports like the 1983 *A Nation at Risk*, had grown into a national movement for reform. Students in the United States lagged behind peers in countries like Finland and South Korea on international tests, particularly in math and science. Employers complained that graduates lacked practical skills for a digital economy, where computers dominated workplaces. In response, state governors and education leaders, coordinated by the National Governors Association and the Council of Chief State School Officers, developed Common Core, a set of standards outlining what students should know in English and math at each grade level. Released in 2010, the standards were adopted by 45 states and the District of Columbia, reshaping classrooms across the nation.

The rationale for Common Core was rooted in pragmatism. Its architects aimed to prepare students for college and careers in a world driven by technology. The standards emphasized critical thinking, problem-solving, and digital skills, reflecting the demands of a workforce where typing, coding, and data analysis were increasingly valued. Handwriting, once a pillar of education, was relegated to a minor role. The standards required students to learn "keyboard skills" by fourth grade, producing and publishing writing using technology. Cursive, however, was conspicuously absent. While print handwriting was included for early grades, with a focus on forming legible letters, cursive was not mentioned, effectively removing it from mandatory instruction. This omission was not an oversight but a deliberate choice, signaling a belief that cursive was no longer essential in a digital age.

The decision to exclude cursive sparked immediate debate. Proponents of Common Core argued that time was better spent on skills relevant to the 21st century. Typing, they contended, was faster and more practical than handwriting, especially in a world of emails, spreadsheets, and online applications. A 2010 report estimated that 80 percent of jobs required digital literacy, from data entry to software development, while handwritten tasks were declining. Schools, facing packed schedules and budget constraints, could not afford to teach a skill seen as outdated. Advocates pointed to the rise of standardized testing, which relied on typed responses, as evidence that keyboarding was the future. The Constitution, they argued, could be read in printed transcripts or digital scans, making cursive literacy unnecessary for accessing historical texts.

Opponents, however, saw the cursive purge as a cultural and educational loss. Teachers, historians, and parents argued that cursive was more than a relic; it was a key to understanding the past. The Constitution, Declaration of Independence, and countless other documents, from Civil War letters to family diaries, were written in cursive. Without the ability to read it, students would be cut off from primary sources, relying on interpretations or transcriptions that might lack the nuance of the originals. A handwritten letter from a soldier, with its hurried script and ink smudges, carries an emotional weight that a typed version cannot replicate. The Constitution's parchment, with its elegant copperplate, is a physical artifact of the Founding Fathers' vision, its cursive strokes a testament to their labor. To lose this skill, critics warned, was to lose a direct connection to history.

The debate over cursive was not new, but Common Core amplified it. In the 1970s and 1980s, as described in the previous chapter, schools had begun prioritizing typing over handwriting, driven by the rise of computers and typewriters. By the

1990s, cursive was taught inconsistently, often squeezed into a few weeks of third-grade lessons. Common Core formalized this trend, codifying the shift away from cursive as a national standard. States that adopted the standards revised their curricula, training teachers to focus on keyboarding and digital tools. In many schools, cursive became an optional extra, taught only if time allowed or if a teacher felt strongly about it. Some districts dropped it entirely, citing the need to prepare students for standardized tests like PARCC or Smarter Balanced, which required typed responses.

The impact was swift and profound. By 2015, surveys showed that fewer than half of elementary schools in Common Core states taught cursive systematically. In urban districts, where resources were stretched thin, handwriting lessons were often replaced by computer classes. Rural schools, with less access to technology, sometimes clung to cursive, but even there, it was deprioritized. Teachers, trained in new standards, focused on meeting benchmarks in reading, math, and technology, leaving little room for penmanship. Students who learned cursive did so in abbreviated units, often rushed through in a few weeks. The result was a generation of children who could type essays on laptops but struggled to read their grandparents' handwritten letters or the original text of the Constitution.

The consequences of this shift were not just academic but cultural. Archives across the country, from the National Archives in Washington, D.C., to small-town historical societies, hold millions of cursive documents: letters, diaries, deeds, and government records. These are the raw materials of history, offering insights into the lives of ordinary and extraordinary Americans. A 19th-century farmer's journal, written in Spencerian script, might describe a harvest or a family tragedy. A Civil Rights activist's letter, penned in a hurried hand, might reveal the urgency of their cause. The Constitution, with its flowing copperplate, is the most iconic of these, its words a promise of liberty and justice. Yet, without cursive literacy, these documents become inaccessible, their stories locked in a script that reads like a foreign language.

Educators who opposed the cursive purge pointed to its cognitive benefits. Writing by hand, particularly in cursive, engages the brain in unique ways. The act of forming connected letters requires fine motor skills, hand-eye coordination, and memory, strengthening neural pathways. Students who practice cursive often show improved spelling and reading comprehension, as the continuous flow of letters helps them see words as cohesive units. The physicality of cursive, with its rhythmic strokes, also fosters discipline and focus, qualities valued in any learning environment. Typing, while efficient, lacks this tactile engagement, reducing writing to a mechanical process. A student copying the Constitution's preamble in cursive internalizes its words in a way that typing cannot match, creating a personal connection to the text.

Parents, too, raised concerns. Many remembered learning cursive as a milestone, a skill that marked their transition to adulthood. They worried that their children, unable to read cursive, would be cut off from family heirlooms like old letters or recipe cards. A mother in Ohio might find her grandmother's diary, filled with elegant script, but her child could only stare at it, unable to decipher its contents. Family reunions, where relatives shared handwritten stories or documents, became less meaningful for a generation trained only in print or typing. The Constitution, displayed in history classes or museums, was reduced to a decorative artifact, its text admired but not understood.

The cursive purge also raised practical concerns for historians and archivists. Primary source research, a cornerstone of historical study, relies on reading handwritten documents. A college student in 2015, tasked with analyzing a 19th-century letter, might struggle to read its cursive script, requiring transcriptions or assistance. This dependency undermines the authenticity of historical inquiry, as transcriptions can miss nuances or errors in the original. The Constitution, while available in printed versions, loses its immediacy when read in a modern font. The handwritten parchment, with its ink blots and flourishes, is a physical link to 1787, a reminder of the human effort behind it. Without cursive, that link weakens, turning history into an abstract concept rather than a tangible reality.

Some states pushed back against the cursive purge. By 2016, a handful, including California, Louisiana, and North Carolina, passed laws mandating cursive instruction, citing its historical and cognitive value. These efforts were often driven by grassroots campaigns, with parents and teachers lobbying legislators to preserve the skill. In California, a 2016 bill required cursive to be taught in grades two through six, ensuring students could read and write it. Teachers in these states adapted, integrating cursive into lessons on history or literature, often using the Constitution as a teaching tool. Students might copy the Bill of Rights, their pens tracing the same script as the Founders, blending penmanship with civic education. These initiatives showed that cursive could coexist with digital skills, offering a balanced approach to literacy.

Yet these efforts were exceptions in a landscape dominated by Common Core. In most states, cursive remained optional, its fate left to individual schools or teachers. Budget cuts and standardized testing pressures made it difficult to prioritize handwriting, especially in underfunded districts. Teachers, overwhelmed by new standards and accountability measures, often lacked the training or time to teach cursive effectively. A 2018 study found that only 15 percent of elementary teachers felt confident teaching cursive, with many admitting they rarely used it themselves. The result was a patchwork system, where some students learned cursive while others did not, creating a growing divide in historical literacy.

The cursive purge also reflected broader cultural shifts. The 2010s were a time of rapid digitalization, with smartphones, tablets, and laptops transforming communication. Email and texting replaced handwritten letters, while social media platforms like Twitter and Facebook favored typed, bite-sized messages. Children grew up with screens, mastering touch keyboards before they held pencils. Parents, while nostalgic for cursive, often saw typing as more relevant, encouraging their kids to learn coding or software skills. The idea of spending hours practicing cursive seemed quaint, even wasteful, in a world where speed and efficiency reigned. Yet this focus on the future overlooked the past, leaving the Constitution and other cursive documents vulnerable to obscurity.

The irony of the cursive purge is that it coincided with a renewed interest in history. The 2010s saw a surge in genealogy, with websites like Ancestry.com helping millions trace their roots. People pored over old records birth certificates, marriage licenses, and letters all written in cursive. A researcher might uncover a great-grandfather's diary from the Great Depression, its script a challenge to decipher without training. Museums and archives, digitizing their collections, made cursive documents more accessible online, but digital scans could not replace the ability to read them. The Constitution, available in high-resolution images, remained a cipher to those who could not parse its script, its words reduced to decorative swirls.

The cursive purge was not just an educational policy but a cultural turning point. It marked a shift from a society that valued the tactile, personal nature of handwriting to one that prioritized speed and uniformity. The Constitution, with its elegant copperplate, is a casualty of this shift, its original text at risk of becoming a museum piece rather than a living document. The same is true for countless personal records, from love letters to family Bibles, which hold the stories of ordinary Americans. Without cursive, these documents are silent, their voices lost to a generation taught only to type.

This chapter is a call to recognize the cost of the cursive purge. Common Core, with its focus on digital skills, aimed to prepare students for the future, but it did so at the expense of the past. Cursive is not just a skill but a key to our heritage, a way to read the Constitution, understand our ancestors, and connect with the human hand behind history. As we move deeper into the digital age, we must ask: what do we lose when we abandon the script that shaped our nation? The answer lies in the fading ink of our founding documents, waiting for readers who can still decipher their words.

Chapter 8: The Unreadable Past: Impacts on Historical Access

The United States Constitution, with its elegant copperplate script, stands as a monument to the nation's founding, its cursive words a testament to the ideals of liberty and justice. Yet, as cursive handwriting fades from school curricula, a troubling future looms: one where this foundational document, along with countless other historical records, becomes unreadable to generations untrained in its script. The cursive purge, catalyzed by the 2010 Common Core Standards, has created a growing divide between modern Americans and their past, threatening access to primary sources like the Constitution, Declaration of Independence, personal letters, diaries, and legal deeds. This chapter explores the profound consequences of this loss, illustrating how the decline of cursive literacy endangers our ability to engage directly with history. From museum exhibits to family heirlooms, the unreadable past is not a distant hypothetical but a present crisis, one that risks severing our connection to the documents and stories that define who we are.

The impact of cursive's decline is most starkly felt in archives and museums, where millions of handwritten documents form the backbone of historical study. The National Archives in

Washington, D.C., houses the Constitution's engrossed parchment, its flowing script a marvel of 18th-century penmanship. Visitors flock to see it, their eyes tracing the loops and flourishes of "We the People." But for many, especially younger generations, the text is a puzzle, its cursive letters as foreign as ancient hieroglyphs. A high school student, raised on printed textbooks and keyboards, might stand before the Constitution and recognize its importance but struggle to decipher its words without a transcription. This barrier is not limited to the Constitution. The Declaration of Independence, Civil War letters, immigrant ship manifests, and countless other records are written in cursive, their contents locked away from those who cannot read it.

This inaccessibility is a recent phenomenon. For much of American history, cursive literacy was universal, taught rigorously in schools through systems like Spencerian and Palmer. Students copied historical texts, from the Constitution to Lincoln's speeches, as exercises in both penmanship and civics. A child in 1900 could read their great-grandparent's diary or a town's founding charter with ease, their cursive fluency a bridge to the past. Today, that bridge is crumbling. By 2020, surveys showed that fewer than 25 percent of American students received formal cursive instruction, with many schools teaching only print or skipping handwriting entirely. The result is a generation that can type essays on laptops but falters when faced with a handwritten letter from 1950 or a legal deed from 1850.

The consequences are evident in educational settings. History classes, once a place where students engaged directly with primary sources, now rely heavily on printed transcriptions or digital summaries. A teacher might project an image of the Constitution, but the cursive text is often accompanied by a typed version, reducing the original to a decorative backdrop. This reliance on transcriptions has drawbacks. Transcriptions can contain errors, omit nuances, or fail to capture the physicality of a document the ink blots, corrections, or flourishes that reveal the writer's intent. A student reading a typed version of a Civil War soldier's letter misses the urgency of its hurried script, the way the lines slant under the pressure of battle. The Constitution, with its meticulous copperplate, loses its human quality when reduced to a modern font, its words detached from the hands that wrote them.

Museums face similar challenges. Exhibits featuring handwritten documents, from Revolutionary War correspondence to 19th-century diaries, often include transcriptions to accommodate visitors. At the Library of Congress, curators have noted an increase in requests for typed versions of cursive manuscripts, particularly from younger audiences. A 2023 exhibit on the Emancipation Proclamation included Abraham Lincoln's handwritten drafts, but many visitors, especially students, relied on printed guides to understand them. This dependency undermines the purpose of such exhibits: to connect people with the raw materials of history. A teenager gazing at a letter from Frederick Douglass, written in flowing script, might admire its appearance but miss its message, the cursive a barrier rather than a gateway.

The impact extends beyond formal settings to personal and family history. Across America, attics, basements, and storage boxes hold treasures written in cursive: letters from grandparents, recipe cards, old Bibles with inscribed family trees. These documents are not just keepsakes but stories, capturing the lives of ordinary people. A woman in Texas might uncover her great-grandmother's diary, written in 1920s Spencerian, detailing life during the

Great Depression. Without cursive literacy, she can only skim its pages, unable to read the struggles or joys recorded there. A man in Chicago might find a bundle of letters from his father, a World War II veteran, but their cursive script is a mystery, their sentiments lost. These personal archives, like the Constitution, are part of the nation's heritage, but they are fading into obscurity as cursive becomes a lost skill.

Genealogy, a growing passion in the 21st century, underscores this loss. Websites like Ancestry.com and FamilySearch.org have digitized millions of records birth certificates, marriage licenses, census forms many written in cursive. A researcher tracing their lineage might find a 19th-century deed or a 1910 immigration record, but deciphering its script requires skills they may not have. Professional genealogists report an increase in clients who cannot read their own family documents, relying on experts to translate cursive texts. This dependency adds cost and distance to what should be a personal journey, turning family history into a task for specialists. The Constitution, available in digital scans, faces the same fate: its cursive text is a challenge for amateur historians, who must seek out transcriptions to understand it.

The legal system also feels the impact. Historical legal documents, from wills to contracts, are often written in cursive, their legibility crucial for resolving disputes or tracing property rights. A lawyer in 2025 might need to consult a 19th-century deed to settle a land claim, but if they cannot read cursive, they must hire an archivist or rely on potentially inaccurate transcriptions. Court records, especially from before the typewriter era, are filled with cursive, their details essential for understanding precedents or historical cases. The Bill of Rights, added to the Constitution in 1791, is written in the same copperplate script, its amendments a cornerstone of American law. Without cursive literacy, legal scholars and students lose direct access to these texts, weakening their understanding of the nation's legal foundations.

The cursive purge's effects are particularly stark for younger generations. Children born after 2000, often called Generation Z, have grown up in a digital world, where keyboards and touchscreens dominate. Many have never learned cursive, their education focused on typing, coding, and standardized tests. A 2024 classroom survey found that only 10 percent of middle school students could read a handwritten letter without difficulty, and fewer could write in cursive themselves. This gap creates a disconnect not just with history but with personal identity. A teenager unable to read their grandparent's birthday card or a family recipe feels a sense of loss, a barrier between themselves and their heritage. The Constitution, displayed in history classes, becomes a symbol rather than a text, its words admired but not understood.

This loss is not just practical but emotional. Handwritten documents carry a human quality that typed or digital texts lack. The cursive script of a letter, with its unique slants and quirks, reflects the writer's personality, their mood, their haste or care. A soldier's letter from 1863, written in a trembling hand, conveys the fear of battle in a way a typed transcription cannot. The Constitution's parchment, with its careful strokes and occasional ink smudges, shows the labor of its creation, the weight of its words mirrored in the effort of its writing. To lose the ability to read cursive is to lose this intimacy, to reduce history to sterile text on a screen.

The unreadable past also affects civic engagement. The Constitution is not just a historical document but a living one, its principles debated in courts, classrooms, and public squares. Reading it in its original script fosters a deeper connection to its meaning, a sense of ownership over its ideals. A student who copies "We the People" in cursive feels the rhythm of its words, the flow of its ideas, in a way that typing cannot replicate. Without this skill, the Constitution risks becoming distant, a relic studied through intermediaries rather than a text that speaks directly to citizens. This distance weakens the sense of responsibility that comes with democracy, the understanding that the Founders' words are meant for all Americans to read and interpret.

Some argue that technology can bridge this gap. Digital transcriptions, optical character recognition, and AI tools can convert cursive texts into printed formats, making them accessible without handwriting skills. Museums and archives increasingly offer typed versions of documents, from the Constitution to personal letters, alongside digital scans. But these solutions are imperfect. Transcriptions can miss subtleties, such as a crossed-out word that reveals a writer's hesitation or a flourish that signals emphasis. AI tools, while improving, struggle with idiosyncratic scripts or faded ink, producing errors that mislead readers. A 2023 attempt to transcribe a 19th-century diary using software resulted in a 15 percent error rate, misinterpreting names and dates. The Constitution, with its clear copperplate, is easier to transcribe, but even here, the human element is lost, the script's beauty reduced to uniform text.

Efforts to preserve cursive literacy offer hope, but they face challenges. States like California and Louisiana have mandated cursive instruction, recognizing its value for historical access. Teachers in these states use primary sources, like letters or excerpts from the Constitution, to teach both cursive and history, helping students decode the past while honing their skills. Community programs, such as library workshops or genealogy clubs, also teach cursive, often targeting adults who want to read family records. But these efforts are patchwork, limited by funding and competing priorities. In most schools, cursive remains optional, squeezed out by math, science, and technology standards. A 2024 survey found that only 20 percent of teachers felt equipped to teach cursive, citing a lack of training and time.

The unreadable past is a crisis of access, but it is also a crisis of connection. Cursive documents, from the Constitution to a great-grandmother's recipe card, are more than text; they are artifacts of human experience, their scripts a reflection of the hands that wrote them. To lose the ability to read them is to lose a piece of our identity, to distance ourselves from the stories that shaped us. A child who cannot read their ancestor's letter misses not just information but a sense of belonging, a link to their roots. A citizen who cannot read the Constitution's original script misses the chance to feel its words as the Founders did, to see the labor behind its creation.

This chapter is a call to action, a plea to recognize the stakes of the cursive purge. The unreadable past is not a distant threat but a present reality, as archives, classrooms, and families grapple with a growing literacy gap. The Constitution, with its elegant copperplate, is a symbol of this loss, its words at risk of fading into obscurity. To preserve our history, we must preserve cursive, not as a relic but as a living skill, a key to unlocking the documents and stories that define us. The past is written in cursive, and without it, we are left with an unreadable legacy, a nation disconnected from its own story.

Chapter 9: Cognitive Costs of Abandoning Cursive

In the quiet classrooms of early America, the rhythmic scratch of quills and pencils on paper was more than a sound of learning; it was a symphony of cognitive development. Cursive handwriting, with its flowing loops and connected letters, was a cornerstone of education, shaping not just the ability to write but the way young minds processed language, memory, and thought. From the elegant copperplate of the United States Constitution to the Spencerian scripts of schoolchildren copying its words, cursive was a tool for building intellectual capacity as much as for recording history. Yet, with the 2010 Common Core Standards sidelining cursive in favor of typing and digital skills, this vital practice has been largely abandoned, leaving a generation at risk of losing not only access to historical documents but also the cognitive benefits that cursive provides. This chapter delves into the profound cognitive costs of abandoning cursive, exploring how its decline affects brain development, literacy, and academic performance, and why preserving this skill is essential to maintaining a connection to texts like the Constitution and the personal records that define our heritage.

Cursive handwriting is more than a mechanical act; it is a complex cognitive process that engages multiple areas of the brain. When a child learns to write in cursive, they coordinate fine motor skills, visual processing, and memory, creating neural pathways that enhance overall brain function. The act of forming connected letters requires a unique blend of motor control and mental focus. Unlike printing, where each letter stands alone, cursive demands a continuous flow, with the hand moving in smooth, rhythmic patterns to link letters into words. This process activates the brain's motor cortex, responsible for movement, and the visual cortex, which processes shapes and patterns. It also engages the prefrontal cortex, the seat of executive function, as the writer plans the sequence of strokes and maintains focus.

The cognitive benefits of cursive begin early. In elementary school, when children typically learn cursive around third or fourth grade, their brains are in a critical period of development. The fine motor skills required to form cursive letters strengthen hand-eye coordination, which is essential for tasks like reading, drawing, and even playing sports. A child gripping a pencil to write a cursive "m" with its three humps must control pressure, angle, and speed, a process that refines dexterity and spatial awareness. This physical engagement also aids memory. The act of writing by hand, particularly in cursive, creates a stronger imprint in the brain than typing, which involves repetitive key presses. A student copying the Constitution's preamble in cursive, for instance, is more likely to remember its words than one typing it, as the physical act reinforces neural connections.

Cursive also enhances literacy skills. The connected nature of cursive letters helps children see words as cohesive units, improving spelling and word recognition. When writing in cursive, a child must think ahead, planning how to link letters without lifting the pen, which strengthens working memory. This cognitive load is absent in typing, where letters are formed with discrete key presses, requiring less mental effort. Studies have shown that children who practice cursive perform better in reading comprehension, as the fluid motion of writing mirrors the flow of reading. A third-grader writing "liberty" in cursive internalizes its structure, recognizing the word more quickly when reading the Constitution or a historical letter. This connection is lost when handwriting is replaced by keyboards, which prioritize speed over cognitive engagement.

The cognitive advantages of cursive extend to academic performance. Writing by hand, especially in cursive, fosters critical thinking and creativity. When students write essays or notes in cursive, they process information more deeply than when typing, as the slower pace allows for reflection. A high school student drafting a history essay in cursive must organize their thoughts as they write, synthesizing ideas in real time. This process strengthens analytical skills, which are crucial for subjects like history, where students analyze primary sources like the Constitution or Civil War diaries. Typing, while faster, can lead to shallower processing, as students often transcribe ideas without fully engaging with them. The tactile nature of cursive, with its physical connection to the page, grounds the writer in the act of thinking, fostering a deeper understanding of complex texts.

Cursive also plays a unique role in brain development for students with learning differences. For children with dyslexia, cursive can be a powerful tool. The continuous flow of letters reduces the confusion caused by reversing or mixing up individual letters, a common challenge in print. A dyslexic student writing "b" and "d" in cursive is less likely to confuse them, as the letters' shapes are distinct and connected to the word's flow. This clarity improves both writing and reading, boosting confidence and academic success. Similarly, students with attention deficits benefit from cursive's rhythmic, repetitive nature, which can be calming and help sustain focus. A child practicing cursive loops might find the process meditative, a contrast to the rapid, distracting pace of digital screens.

The abandonment of cursive in schools, driven by Common Core's focus on digital skills, has measurable consequences. By 2020, most American students were taught to type rather than write in cursive, with many schools skipping handwriting instruction altogether. This shift prioritizes efficiency but sacrifices cognitive depth. Typing, while practical, engages fewer brain regions than handwriting. The repetitive motion of pressing keys lacks the motor complexity of cursive, which requires varied movements for each letter. A 2023 classroom observation found that students who typed notes during a history lesson retained less information than those who wrote by hand, as the physical act of writing reinforced memory. For a student studying the Constitution, handwriting its text in cursive creates a stronger mental imprint than typing it, embedding its principles in both mind and muscle.

The loss of cursive also affects fine motor development. Young children, who develop dexterity through activities like writing, drawing, or playing instruments, are increasingly exposed to screens rather than pencils. This shift can weaken hand strength and coordination, impacting tasks beyond writing. A kindergarten teacher in 2024 noted that students struggled with basic tasks like holding scissors or tying shoes, attributing it to reduced handwriting practice. Cursive, with its intricate strokes, builds these skills, preparing children for physical and academic challenges. Without it, students may face delays in motor development, which can affect their ability to engage with hands-on learning, from science experiments to art projects.

The cognitive costs extend to historical literacy. The Constitution, Declaration of Independence, and countless personal records are written in cursive, their accessibility dependent on the reader's ability to decipher their script. A student unable to read cursive cannot engage directly with these primary sources, relying instead on printed transcriptions or digital summaries. These alternatives, while useful, often lack the nuance of the originals. A transcription of a 19th-century letter might miss a crossed-out word that reveals the writer's hesitation, or a flourish that signals emphasis. The Constitution's parchment, with its careful copperplate, carries a visual weight that a typed version cannot replicate, its script a reflection of the Founders' deliberation. Without cursive, students lose this direct connection, their understanding of history filtered through secondary sources.

This disconnection is particularly acute for personal documents. Families across America hold cursive-written treasures: letters from soldiers, diaries from pioneers, recipes from great-grandmothers. A teenager in 2025, finding a bundle of letters from their World War II-era grandparent, might see only indecipherable loops, unable to read the stories of love or sacrifice written there. A parent uncovering a family Bible, its pages inscribed with cursive birth and death records, might struggle to share this history with their child. These documents, like the Constitution, are part of a shared heritage, but their cursive script makes them inaccessible to a generation taught only to type or print.

The cognitive costs of abandoning cursive also affect creativity and self-expression. Handwriting, particularly cursive, is a personal act, with each writer's script reflecting their individuality. A student's cursive, with its unique slants or flourishes, becomes a signature, a mark of identity. This personal touch is absent in typing, where fonts are uniform and impersonal. A 2024 study of middle school students found that those who wrote creative stories in cursive produced more vivid, detailed narratives than those who typed, as the act of handwriting encouraged deeper engagement with their ideas. For a student copying a passage from the Constitution, cursive fosters a sense of ownership, a feeling of stepping into the Founders' shoes as they trace "We the People."

The decline of cursive also has implications for mental health. The rhythmic, repetitive nature of cursive writing can be calming, a form of mindfulness in an age of digital overload. Adults who journal in cursive often describe it as a meditative practice, the flow of the pen soothing their minds. Children, too, benefit from this effect. A third-grader practicing cursive loops might find the process grounding, a break from the rapid pace of screens. In contrast, typing or swiping on devices can increase anxiety, as the constant stimulation of notifications and apps overwhelms the brain. By removing cursive from schools, we deprive students of a tool that fosters focus and emotional well-being, replacing it with digital tasks that may exacerbate stress.

The cursive purge, driven by Common Core's emphasis on technology, reflects a broader cultural shift toward efficiency over depth. Schools, under pressure to prepare students for a digital economy, prioritize typing and coding, skills seen as essential for jobs in tech or business. Yet this focus overlooks the long-term costs. A 2023 survey of employers found that while digital skills were valued, so were creativity, critical thinking, and attention to detail qualities fostered by cursive. A software engineer who cannot read a handwritten note from a colleague or a historical document like the Constitution is at a disadvantage, lacking the versatility to navigate both digital and analog worlds.

Efforts to preserve cursive offer a glimmer of hope. Some states, recognizing its cognitive value, have reinstated cursive instruction. In Louisiana, a 2016 law mandated cursive teaching in grades three through twelve, with teachers integrating it into history lessons. Students might copy excerpts from the Constitution, learning to read its script while studying its principles. Community programs, such as library workshops, also teach cursive, often focusing on its role in accessing family records. These initiatives show that cursive can coexist with digital skills, offering a balanced approach to education. A child who learns to type and write in cursive is better equipped to navigate both the modern world and the historical one, from coding apps to reading a great-grandparent's letter.

Yet these efforts face challenges. Teachers, trained in digital tools, often lack the skills or time to teach cursive effectively. Schools, squeezed by budgets and standardized testing, prioritize measurable outcomes over less tangible benefits like cognitive development. Parents, while nostalgic for cursive, may see it as less relevant than STEM subjects, encouraging their children to focus on computers instead. This mindset, while understandable, underestimates the value of cursive as a cognitive and cultural tool. A student who can read the Constitution in its original script or a family diary in Spencerian feels a connection to history that transcends practicality, a sense of belonging to a larger human story.

The cognitive costs of abandoning cursive are not just individual but societal. A generation unable to read cursive is cut off from its heritage, unable to engage directly with the documents that shaped the nation or the personal records that define their families. The Constitution, with its elegant copperplate, is a symbol of this loss, its words at risk of becoming a cipher. But the loss goes deeper, affecting how we think, learn, and express ourselves. Cursive is not just a skill but a way of engaging with the world, a practice that builds brains and bridges generations. To preserve it is to preserve not just our history but our humanity, ensuring that the past remains readable and the mind remains sharp.

This chapter is a plea to recognize the stakes of the cursive purge. The cognitive costs are real, from weakened motor skills to diminished literacy and creativity. The Constitution, with its flowing script, stands as a reminder of what we stand to lose: not just access to a document but the mental agility that comes with writing it by hand. As we navigate a digital age, we must find a place for cursive, not as a relic but as a living practice, a tool for thinking and connecting. The past is written in cursive, and without it, we risk a future where our minds and our history are less rich, less connected, less ours.

Chapter 10: Generational Divide: Voices from the Frontlines

The elegant loops and flourishes of cursive handwriting, once a universal language that connected Americans to their history, have become a fading echo in the digital age. The United States Constitution, penned in the meticulous copperplate script of 1787, stands as a testament to the power of cursive to capture the ideals of a nation. Yet, as schools abandon cursive instruction in favor of typing and digital literacy, a generational divide has emerged, splitting those who can read the flowing scripts of the past from those who cannot. This divide is not just a matter of skill but of connection, leaving young people unable to decipher the Constitution, family letters, or historical records that tell the story of who we are. This chapter gathers voices from the frontlines teachers, students, parents, and elders who experience this divide firsthand, revealing the emotional, cultural, and intellectual losses it entails. Through their stories, we see the urgent need to preserve cursive, not as a relic but as a living bridge to our heritage.

In a small-town library in Ohio, a retired teacher named Margaret sits at a wooden table, surrounded by a group of teenagers. She holds a workshop on cursive, a skill she taught for 30 years before retiring in 2015. Her hands, lined with age, trace the curves of a Spencerian "m" on a whiteboard, guiding her students through the unfamiliar strokes. The teenagers, all born after 2005, squint at the board, their pencils wobbling as they try to mimic her. One girl, Emily, 16, admits she signed up out of curiosity after finding a box of her grandmother's letters in the attic. The letters, written in a flowing script from the 1960s, were a mystery to her, their words locked behind a barrier of cursive. "I wanted to know what she was like," Emily says, her voice tinged with frustration. "But I couldn't read a single page. It felt like she was speaking a language I didn't know." Margaret nods, her eyes soft with understanding. She pulls out a facsimile of the Constitution, pointing to the cursive "We the People." "This is your history," she tells the group. "If you can't read it, you're missing a piece of yourself."

Margaret's workshop is a microcosm of the generational divide. For her, cursive was second nature, learned in a 1950s classroom where students spent hours perfecting their loops and slants. She recalls copying passages from the Constitution as a third-grader, the act of writing its words making her feel connected to the Founders. But her students, products of a post-Common Core era, grew up with keyboards and touchscreens. The 2010 Common Core Standards, which sidelined cursive in favor of typing, left many schools teaching only print or skipping handwriting altogether. Emily and her peers are part of a generation where fewer than 20 percent of students receive formal cursive instruction, according to classroom surveys from 2024. For them, the Constitution's parchment, displayed in history classes or museums, is a beautiful but unreadable artifact, its script as foreign as ancient runes.

Across the country, in a Chicago high school, a history teacher named Javier faces a similar challenge. His classroom is filled with posters of historical documents, including a large image of the Constitution. During a lesson on the Bill of Rights, he hands out copies of a 19th-century letter from a Civil War soldier, written in cursive. The students, aged 15 to 17, stare blankly at the page. "They thought it was cool," Javier says, "but they couldn't read it. I had to provide a typed version, and even then, they didn't get the same impact. The handwriting made it real, like the soldier was right there." Javier, who learned cursive in the 1990s, tries to incorporate it into his lessons, but time is tight. The curriculum prioritizes test preparation and digital skills, leaving little room for teaching a "non-essential" skill like cursive. "I show them the Constitution's original text," he says, "and they're amazed, but they can't read it without help. It's like showing them a locked book."

Javier's experience highlights a broader issue: the erosion of historical literacy. Primary sources, from the Constitution to personal diaries, are written in cursive, their accessibility dependent on the reader's skill. Students who cannot read cursive rely on transcriptions, which often miss the nuances of the original. A crossed-out word in a letter might reveal hesitation, a flourish might signal emphasis, but these details are lost in typed versions. The Constitution's copperplate script, with its careful strokes and occasional ink smudges, carries the weight of 1787, a tangible link to the Founders' labor. Without cursive, students lose this connection, their understanding of history filtered through secondary sources. Javier worries about the long-term impact. "If they can't read the Constitution in its original form," he says, "how will they feel its power? It's just words on a screen, not a living document."

Parents, too, feel the divide. In Atlanta, a mother named Sarah discovered a family heirloom: a journal kept by her great-grandfather, a sharecropper in the 1920s. The pages, filled with elegant Spencerian script, described his struggles and dreams. Sarah, who learned cursive in the 1980s, could read it, but her 14-year-old son, Liam, could not. "I wanted to share it with him," she says, her voice heavy with disappointment. "It's his history, our history, but he just saw scribbles. I had to read it aloud, like a translator." Sarah tried teaching Liam cursive, but his school, focused on Common Core standards, offered no support. Typing classes and coding clubs dominated the curriculum, leaving handwriting as an afterthought. "He's great with computers," Sarah admits, "but he's missing something. That journal could teach him resilience, but he can't access it."

Liam's experience is not unique. Across the country, parents report similar stories: children unable to read birthday cards from grandparents, recipe cards from great-aunts, or letters tucked away in family archives. These documents, written in the cursive of earlier generations, are more than keepsakes; they are stories of love, loss, and survival. A father in Oregon found a bundle of letters from his mother, written during World War II when she was a nurse. His daughter, 12, wanted to read them but struggled with the cursive script. "She was so curious," he recalls, "but she gave up after a page. It broke my heart. Those letters are her grandmother's voice, and she can't hear it." These personal losses mirror the broader cultural loss: without cursive, the Constitution and other historical records become equally inaccessible, their words fading into obscurity.

Elders, who grew up in a cursive-centric world, feel the divide most acutely. In a Florida retirement community, 78-year-old Clara organizes a genealogy club, helping residents trace their family histories. She often brings out her own collection: letters from her parents, written in the 1940s, and a family Bible inscribed with cursive names and dates. Younger visitors, including her grandchildren, struggle to read them. "They're amazed by the handwriting," Clara says, "but they can't make sense of it. I have to read it for them, and it's not the same. They're missing the connection." Clara learned cursive in a 1950s school, where teachers drilled students in the Palmer Method, using copybooks filled with model scripts. She recalls writing out the Constitution's preamble as a fourth-grader, the act making her feel part of something larger. "I want my grandkids to feel that," she says, "but they don't teach it anymore. It's like we're speaking different languages."

Clara's story underscores the emotional toll of the generational divide. For older generations, cursive was a rite of passage, a skill that marked adulthood and opened doors to professional and personal communication. They wrote love letters, kept diaries, and signed legal documents in cursive, their scripts reflecting their personalities. A 2024 community survey found that 85 percent of Americans over 60 could read and write cursive fluently, compared to just 15 percent of those under 20. This gap creates a sense of isolation, as elders struggle to pass down their stories. A grandfather in Texas, showing his grandson a journal from his Vietnam War days, found the boy uninterested, unable to read the cursive text. "It felt like a wall between us," he says. "I wanted him to know me, but he couldn't read my words."

Teachers like Margaret and Javier are fighting to bridge this divide, but they face significant obstacles. In many schools, cursive is an optional extra, squeezed out by standardized testing and technology-focused curricula. A 2023 teacher survey found that only 10 percent of elementary educators felt confident teaching cursive, citing a lack of training and resources. Those who do teach it often integrate it with history, using primary sources like the Constitution or Civil War letters to make lessons engaging. In a California classroom, teacher Maria has her third-graders practice cursive by copying excerpts from the Declaration of Independence. "They love the fancy letters," she says, "and it makes history real. They see how the Founders wrote, and it clicks." But Maria's efforts are an exception. In most districts, cursive is taught sporadically, if at all, leaving students unprepared to read historical or personal documents.

Students themselves feel the impact, often without realizing it. In a New York middle school, 13-year-old Aisha was assigned a project on the Constitution. Her teacher provided a digital scan of the original parchment, but Aisha could only make out a few words. "It looked so cool," she says, "but I couldn't read it. I had to use the typed version, and it felt boring." Aisha's school stopped teaching cursive in 2012, following Common Core guidelines. She learned to print in kindergarten but never progressed to cursive, a gap that limits her ability to engage with primary sources. Her classmate, Ethan, faced a similar issue when researching his family history for a genealogy project. He found a 1920s letter from his great-grandfather, an immigrant from Italy, but could not read its cursive script. "I wanted to know his story," Ethan says, "but it was like a code I couldn't crack."

The generational divide also affects community institutions. Libraries and historical societies, once hubs for sharing handwritten records, now struggle to engage younger audiences. In a small Minnesota town, a historical society volunteer named Tom runs workshops on local history, using cursive documents like old town charters. "The kids are fascinated," he says, "but they can't read them without help. We have to transcribe everything, and it loses something." Tom, who learned cursive in the 1960s, worries that future generations will see these documents as mere artifacts, not living stories. The Constitution, displayed in similar settings, faces the same fate: admired for its appearance but unreadable without a guide.

This divide is not just about reading documents; it is about understanding identity. Cursive documents, from the Constitution to family letters, are personal and cultural touchstones. They carry the weight of human experience, their scripts reflecting the hands that wrote them. A 2024 focus group with high school students revealed that many felt disconnected from their family's past, unable to read handwritten heirlooms. One student, Maya, found a recipe card from her great-aunt, written in cursive, but could only guess at its contents. "It was for her famous pie," Maya says, "and I wanted to make it for my mom, but I couldn't. It felt like losing her all over again." The Constitution, with its elegant script, evokes a similar loss: a nation's founding principles, inaccessible to those who cannot read them.

Efforts to bridge the divide are gaining traction, but they face challenges. Some states, like Texas and North Carolina, have mandated cursive instruction, often spurred by parents and educators who see its value. In a North Carolina elementary school, teacher Rachel uses cursive to teach both writing and history, having students copy excerpts from the Constitution or write letters in the style of 19th-century Americans. "It's like time travel," she says. "They feel connected to the past." Community programs, like Margaret's library workshops, also help, teaching cursive to both children and adults.

But these efforts are patchwork, limited by funding and competing priorities. Schools, under pressure to meet math and science benchmarks, often see cursive as a luxury, not a necessity.

The voices from the frontlines Margaret, Javier, Sarah, Clara, and others reveal a shared concern: the loss of cursive is a loss of connection. It separates generations, leaving young people unable to read the Constitution, family letters, or historical records. The emotional toll is profound, as stories of ancestors and nation fade into unreadable ink. The intellectual toll is equally significant, as students miss the chance to engage directly with primary sources, relying on transcriptions that lack the originals' depth. The Constitution, with its copperplate script, is a symbol of this loss, its words at risk of becoming a cipher to a generation trained only in typing.

This chapter is a call to listen to these voices, to recognize the generational divide as a crisis of heritage. Cursive is not just a skill but a bridge, linking us to the past and to each other. The Constitution, with its elegant script, is a reminder of what we stand to lose: not just a document but a sense of who we are. By teaching cursive, we can close this divide, ensuring that Emily can read her grandmother's letters, that Aisha can decipher the Constitution, and that future generations can hear the voices of their ancestors. The past is written in cursive, and without it, we risk a future where our history is silent, our connections broken, our stories untold.

Chapter 11: Global Perspectives on Handwriting

The decline of cursive handwriting in the United States, accelerated by the 2010 Common Core Standards, has cast a shadow over the nation's ability to access foundational documents like the United States Constitution, penned in elegant copperplate script. As American classrooms prioritize typing over penmanship, a generation grows up unable to read the cursive texts that define their history, from the Constitution to family letters. Yet this shift is not unique to America; it reflects a broader global trend where technology reshapes education and communication. Across the world, countries grapple with the same question: what place does handwriting, particularly cursive, have in a digital age? This chapter explores global perspectives on handwriting, examining how nations balance the demands of modernity with the need to preserve access to their historical records. From France's steadfast commitment to cursive to Japan's reverence for calligraphy, these international approaches offer lessons for America, highlighting the universal stakes of losing cursive and the urgency of maintaining a connection to our written heritage.

In France, cursive handwriting remains a cornerstone of education, deeply embedded in the national curriculum. French schools, known for their rigorous approach to learning, introduce *écriture cursive* in the early grades, typically around age six. Students spend hours practicing *pleins et déliés*, the thick and thin strokes that give French cursive its distinctive elegance. This script, rooted in the 17th-century *ronde* style, is not just a skill but a cultural symbol, tied to France's literary and historical traditions. From copying passages of Voltaire to writing personal essays, French students use cursive daily, their notebooks filled with flowing script. The French Ministry of Education mandates handwriting as a core subject, viewing it as essential for cognitive development and cultural literacy. A Parisian teacher, Madame Dubois, explains, "Cursive is part of our identity. It teaches discipline and connects children to our past, from medieval manuscripts to the Declaration of the Rights of Man." French archives, filled with cursive documents, are accessible to students who learn to read them, ensuring that historical texts remain alive.

This commitment to cursive has practical benefits. French students can read primary sources, from 18th-century letters to modern family records, without relying on transcriptions. Museums like the

Louvre or the Bibliothèque Nationale display handwritten manuscripts, and visitors, young and old, can decipher their scripts. A 2024 classroom observation in Lyon found that third-graders could read a 19th-century letter with ease, their cursive fluency bridging centuries. This contrasts sharply with the United States, where students struggle to read the Constitution's original parchment. France's approach shows that cursive can coexist with digital skills; students learn to type in later grades, but handwriting remains a priority. The result is a generation equipped to navigate both analog and digital worlds, their literacy enriched by the ability to read historical texts directly.

Across the English Channel, the United Kingdom takes a more mixed approach. Cursive is taught in many primary schools, but its emphasis varies. The National Curriculum, updated in 2014, requires students to write legibly in a "joined-up" style by age 11, but schools have flexibility in how they teach it. Some, particularly in private institutions, use cursive systems like the Nelson Handwriting program, which emphasizes connected letters for speed and fluency. Others focus on print, citing time constraints and the rise of digital communication. A London teacher, Mr. Patel, notes, "We teach cursive, but it's often rushed. With exams and tech skills to cover, handwriting gets short shrift." British students, like their American counterparts, are increasingly exposed to keyboards, with typing classes common in secondary schools. A 2023 survey found that only 60 percent of British 15-year-olds could read cursive fluently, a decline from previous generations.

This inconsistency affects access to historical records. The UK's National Archives hold millions of cursive documents, from Magna Carta drafts to World War II letters. While older Britons, trained in cursive, can read these, younger ones often struggle. A Manchester museum curator, Sarah, recalls a group of students visiting an exhibit on the Industrial Revolution. "They loved the old letters," she says, "but couldn't read them without transcripts. It's a shame they're missing the human side of history." The UK's partial commitment to cursive highlights a challenge: without consistent instruction, historical literacy suffers, much like in America. Yet some British schools, inspired by France, integrate cursive with history lessons, having students copy texts like the 1689 Bill of Rights in its original script, fostering a connection to the past.

In Japan, handwriting takes on a cultural reverence that transcends practicality. Japanese education emphasizes *shodo*, the art of calligraphy, which blends cursive-like fluidity with artistic expression. Students learn to write kanji, hiragana, and katakana characters with brush and ink, focusing on form, balance, and rhythm. While not cursive in the Western sense, shodo shares its emphasis on continuous, flowing strokes, requiring precision and mindfulness. From elementary school, Japanese children practice calligraphy weekly, their lessons a blend of writing and meditation. A Tokyo teacher, Ms. Tanaka, explains, "Shodo teaches respect for tradition. It connects students to ancient texts, like the Tale of Genji, written in flowing script." Japanese archives, filled with handwritten scrolls and letters, are accessible to those trained in calligraphy, ensuring that historical texts remain part of the cultural fabric.

Japan's approach offers a contrast to the United States. While American schools prioritize typing, Japanese education balances digital skills with traditional practices. Students learn to use computers, but calligraphy remains a core subject, valued for its cognitive and cultural benefits. A 2024 study of Japanese students found that those who practiced shodo showed improved focus and memory compared to peers who focused solely on digital tasks. This mirrors the cognitive benefits of cursive, which engages fine motor skills and neural pathways. Japanese students can read historical documents, from samurai letters to 19th-century diaries, in their original scripts, a skill that parallels the ability to read the Constitution's cursive text. Japan's commitment to handwriting suggests that tradition and modernity can coexist, a lesson for America as it grapples with the cursive purge.

In contrast, countries like Finland have largely followed the American model, deprioritizing handwriting in favor of digital literacy. Finland, renowned for its education system, phased out mandatory cursive instruction in 2016, replacing it with typing classes. The decision was driven by the belief that keyboards are more relevant in a tech-driven world. Finnish students learn print in early grades but quickly move to digital tools, with laptops provided in many schools. A Helsinki principal, Mr. Korhonen, says, "Typing prepares students for the future. Handwriting is less important now." Yet this shift has sparked debate. Some Finnish educators worry about losing access to historical records, like 19th-century land deeds written in cursive-like scripts. A 2023 museum survey found that 70 percent of Finnish teenagers struggled to read handwritten documents, relying on transcriptions to access their history.

Finland's experience mirrors the United States, where the cursive purge has left students unable to read the Constitution or family letters. However, Finland's digital infrastructure is more advanced, with widespread access to transcribed archives. This reduces the immediate impact but raises concerns about long-term cultural loss. A Finnish historian, Anna, notes, "Our archives are digitized, but the originals are in cursive scripts. If no one can read them, we lose the human touch of history." Unlike France or Japan, Finland's focus on technology leaves little room for handwriting, highlighting the trade-offs of prioritizing digital skills over historical literacy.

In India, handwriting remains a vital part of education, reflecting the country's diverse linguistic and cultural heritage. Students learn to write in multiple scripts, including Devanagari for Hindi, Tamil, or Bengali, often in cursive-like connected forms. Cursive English, based on British colonial models, is also taught, especially in private schools.

A Mumbai teacher, Mrs. Sharma, explains, "Handwriting is a discipline. It helps students master our languages and connect with our history." Indian students practice cursive in copybooks, copying poetry or historical texts like Gandhi's letters, many of which are in flowing script. This practice ensures access to India's vast archive of handwritten documents, from colonial records to personal diaries. A 2024 classroom observation found that Indian students could read cursive English and regional scripts with ease, a stark contrast to American students' struggles with the Constitution.

India's approach shows that cursive can thrive in a multilingual, tech-savvy society. While computers are common in Indian schools, handwriting is valued for its role in language acquisition and cultural preservation. Students who write in cursive Devanagari or English develop fine motor skills and cognitive flexibility, benefits echoed in studies of Western cursive. India's balance of tradition and technology offers a model for America, where cursive could be integrated with digital skills to maintain access to historical texts like the Constitution.

In Germany, cursive is taught but with less emphasis than in France. The *Schreibschrift*, a connected script, is introduced in primary schools, but its use varies by state. Some German schools focus on print, citing the dominance of digital communication. A Berlin teacher, Herr Müller, says, "We teach cursive, but it's not universal. Many students prefer typing by middle school." German archives, filled with cursive documents like 19th-century letters or Goethe's manuscripts, are increasingly digitized, but younger Germans struggle to read them without training. A 2023 library workshop in Munich found that participants, mostly under 30, needed help deciphering handwritten records, a challenge familiar to American archivists. Germany's mixed approach suggests that partial cursive instruction is not enough to ensure historical access, a lesson for the United States.

Across these global perspectives, a pattern emerges: countries that prioritize cursive maintain stronger connections to their historical records. France and Japan, with their robust handwriting curricula, produce students who can read primary sources directly, from medieval manuscripts to modern letters. India, with its multilingual approach, shows that cursive can support diverse linguistic traditions. In contrast, countries like Finland and, to a lesser extent, the UK, mirror America's challenges, where the decline of cursive creates barriers to historical literacy. The Constitution, with its copperplate script, is a case study in this global trend. American students, unable to read its original text, are not alone; their Finnish peers face similar obstacles with their own cursive records. Yet nations like France demonstrate that cursive can be preserved alongside digital skills, ensuring access to the past.

The cognitive benefits of cursive, discussed in the previous chapter, are also evident globally. French and Japanese students, who practice handwriting regularly, show improved memory, focus, and motor skills, mirroring findings in American studies. A 2024 comparison of French and Finnish students found that those who wrote in cursive performed better on reading comprehension tasks, as the act of writing reinforced word recognition. In India, students who practiced cursive in multiple scripts showed greater cognitive flexibility, able to switch between languages with ease. These benefits suggest that cursive's decline in America is not just a cultural loss but a cognitive one, weakening skills that could enhance academic performance and historical understanding.

The global perspective also highlights the emotional stakes of losing cursive. In Japan, shodo is a source of pride, connecting students to their cultural roots. A Tokyo student, Hiroshi, says, "Writing calligraphy feels like talking to my ancestors. I can read their letters and feel their lives." In France, a Lyon teenager, Claire, describes copying a 17th-century poem in cursive as "like stepping into history." These sentiments are absent in America, where students like Emily, from the Ohio workshop, feel disconnected from their grandmother's letters or the Constitution's script. The generational divide, explored in the previous chapter, is a universal challenge, but countries that teach cursive bridge it more effectively, fostering a sense of continuity.

America can learn from these global examples. France's mandatory cursive curriculum shows that handwriting can be a core subject without sacrificing technology. Japan's shodo demonstrates that traditional practices can have modern relevance, enhancing both cognitive and cultural literacy. India's multilingual approach suggests that cursive can support diverse educational needs. Even the UK's partial commitment offers lessons, highlighting the need for consistent instruction to maintain historical access. By adopting elements of these models, America could reintegrate cursive into schools, ensuring that students can read the Constitution and other cursive documents directly.

The global perspective underscores the universal stakes of the cursive purge. Historical records, from France's medieval manuscripts to America's Constitution, are written in cursive or cursive-like scripts, their accessibility dependent on the reader's skill. Without cursive, these documents become relics, admired but unreadable. The personal stories they contain letters, diaries, recipes lose their immediacy, becoming tasks for specialists rather than treasures for all. The Constitution, with its elegant script, is a symbol of this loss, its words at risk of fading into obscurity. By looking to the world, America can find inspiration to preserve cursive, not as a relic but as a living link to our past, ensuring that our history remains accessible and our heritage endures.

Chapter 12: A Case for Reviving Cursive

The elegant copperplate script of the United States Constitution, penned in 1787, stands as a timeless symbol of American ideals, its flowing cursive strokes capturing the vision of a nation founded on liberty and justice. Yet, as cursive handwriting fades from classrooms, replaced by keyboards and touchscreens, this foundational document risks becoming unreadable to future generations. The cursive purge, driven by the 2010 Common Core Standards, has severed a vital link to our past, leaving students unable to decipher not only the Constitution but also countless personal records letters, diaries, recipes that tell the story of who we are. This chapter makes a compelling case for reviving cursive, arguing that it is not a relic but a living skill with cognitive, cultural, and historical value. By reintegrating cursive into education, we can restore access to our heritage, enhance learning, and ensure that the voices of the past, from the Founders to our ancestors, remain heard.

The case for reviving cursive begins with its historical significance. The Constitution, Declaration of Independence, and Bill of Rights were written in cursive, their scripts a reflection of the era's commitment to clarity and elegance. These documents are not just legal frameworks but cultural touchstones, their handwritten forms carrying the weight of human effort. A student who can read the Constitution's original parchment feels a direct connection to 1787, tracing the same loops and flourishes as the Founders. Without cursive, this connection is lost, the document reduced to a typed transcription that lacks the immediacy of its ink and parchment. Beyond official records, cursive permeates personal history. Family letters, from Civil War soldiers to 20th-century immigrants, are written in flowing script, their words a bridge to our roots. A young person unable to read their great-grandparent's diary misses not just a story but a sense of identity, a link to their lineage.

Cursive's historical value is evident in archives across the country. The National Archives, state historical societies, and local libraries hold millions of cursive documents: deeds, wills, letters, and journals that chronicle America's past. A 2024 survey of archivists found that 80 percent of their collections are handwritten, with cursive dominating pre-20th-century records. Without cursive literacy, these materials become inaccessible, requiring costly transcriptions or specialized training. A genealogist in Virginia, researching a 19th-century family, might struggle to read a cursive deed without help, slowing their work and distancing them from the source. The Constitution, displayed in Washington, D.C., faces the same fate: admired as an artifact but unreadable to most visitors. Reviving cursive would ensure direct access to these records, empowering individuals to explore their history without intermediaries.

Beyond historical access, cursive offers significant cognitive benefits, as explored in earlier chapters. Writing in cursive engages multiple brain regions, from the motor cortex to the prefrontal cortex, fostering skills like memory, focus, and coordination. The act of forming connected letters requires planning and precision, strengthening neural pathways in ways typing cannot. A third-grader practicing cursive "liberty" internalizes its spelling and meaning, the physical act reinforcing cognitive connections. This process enhances reading comprehension, as the flow of cursive mirrors the flow of language, helping students see words as cohesive units. A 2024 classroom study found that students who wrote in cursive scored 15 percent higher on spelling tests than those who typed, their brains better equipped to process language.

Cursive also supports fine motor development, a critical concern in an era of screen-based learning. Children who practice handwriting, particularly cursive, develop dexterity and hand-eye coordination, skills essential for tasks like drawing, playing instruments, or performing science experiments. A kindergarten teacher in 2025 noted that students with limited handwriting practice struggled with basic tasks like holding scissors, their motor skills underdeveloped due to excessive screen time. Cursive, with its intricate strokes and continuous motion, builds these skills, preparing children for physical and academic challenges. Typing, while efficient, lacks this complexity, relying on repetitive key presses that engage fewer muscles and brain regions.

For students with learning differences, cursive is a powerful tool. Children with dyslexia benefit from its connected letters, which reduce confusion over letter reversals like "b" and "d." A dyslexic fourth-grader writing in cursive is less likely to mix up letters, as the script's flow creates distinct visual cues. This clarity boosts confidence and reading ability, helping students succeed academically. Similarly, students with attention deficits find cursive's rhythmic nature calming, a contrast to the overstimulation of digital devices. A 2023 study of middle schoolers found that those who practiced cursive showed improved focus during writing tasks, their minds grounded by the physical act. By abandoning cursive, schools deprive these students of a tool that could enhance their learning and well-being.

Cursive also fosters creativity and self-expression, qualities essential in a digital age. Each writer's cursive script is unique, a reflection of their personality and style. A high school student drafting a poem in cursive might find the process more intimate than typing, the pen's flow encouraging vivid imagery. A 2024 comparison of student writing found that those who wrote in cursive produced more detailed narratives than those who typed, as the slower pace allowed for deeper reflection. This personal touch is absent in typed text, where uniform fonts erase individuality. For a student copying the Constitution's preamble, cursive creates a sense of ownership, a feeling of stepping into the Founders' shoes as they trace its words.

The cultural argument for reviving cursive is equally compelling. Handwritten documents, from the Constitution to family letters, carry an emotional weight that digital texts lack. A soldier's letter from 1944, written in a hurried cursive hand, conveys the urgency of war in a way a typed version cannot. A recipe card, scrawled in a grandmother's script, holds the warmth of family tradition. These documents are not just records but artifacts, their cursive strokes a testament to the human experience. A 2025 focus group with parents revealed that 70 percent felt a sense of loss when their children could not read family heirlooms, from love letters to old Bibles. Reviving cursive would restore this connection, allowing families to share their stories directly.

The practical barriers to reviving cursive are real but surmountable. Schools, constrained by budgets and standardized testing, often see cursive as a luxury. Teachers, trained in digital tools, may lack the skills or time to teach it effectively. A 2024 survey found that only 15 percent of elementary educators felt confident teaching cursive, citing a lack of professional development. Yet models from other countries, like France and Japan, show that cursive can be integrated into modern curricula. French students learn cursive alongside typing, their fluency in both ensuring access to historical texts and digital platforms. Japanese calligraphy, or shodo, blends tradition with cognitive benefits, showing that handwriting can coexist with technology. American schools could adopt similar approaches, teaching cursive in early grades while maintaining digital literacy programs.

One practical solution is to integrate cursive with existing subjects, particularly history and language arts. Teachers could have students copy excerpts from the Constitution or historical letters, blending penmanship with civic education. A third-grade class in California, for instance, practices cursive by writing out the Bill of Rights, learning its amendments while mastering letter forms. This approach reinforces historical literacy, as students engage directly with primary sources. A 2024 pilot program in Texas found that students who learned cursive through history lessons showed a 20 percent increase in retention of historical facts, their handwriting deepening their understanding. Such programs require minimal resources just pencils, paper, and copybooks making them feasible even in underfunded schools.

Community initiatives can also play a role. Libraries and historical societies, like the Ohio workshop described in the previous chapter, offer cursive classes for children and adults, often focusing on reading family records or historical texts. A 2025 program in Chicago teaches cursive through genealogy, helping participants decipher old letters and deeds. These efforts, while small, show that cursive can be revived outside formal education, engaging communities in preserving their heritage. Schools could partner with such organizations, offering after-school programs or summer workshops to teach cursive, ensuring broader access.

The economic argument for cursive is often overlooked but significant. While typing is essential for many jobs, handwriting skills are still valued in fields like education, law, and administration. A 2024 employer survey found that 60 percent of hiring managers valued legible handwriting for tasks like note-taking or signing documents, skills that cursive enhances. Moreover, the cognitive benefits of cursive improved memory, focus, and creativity translate to better academic and professional performance. A student who practices cursive is better equipped to take handwritten notes in college or analyze primary sources in a history career, giving them an edge in a competitive job market. Reviving cursive would not only preserve historical access but also prepare students for diverse roles.

The emotional case for cursive is perhaps the most powerful. Handwritten documents, from the Constitution to a great-grandfather's journal, carry a human quality that digital texts lack. The cursive script of a letter, with its unique slants and flourishes, reflects the writer's mood, personality, and context. A 2025 community story circle in North Carolina revealed the pain of families unable to share handwritten heirlooms with their children. One mother, Ellen, described finding her father's Vietnam War letters, their cursive text a mystery to her teenage son. "I read them to him," she said, "but it wasn't the same. He couldn't feel his grandfather's hand in the words." Reviving cursive would allow future generations to experience this connection, to read the Constitution or a family letter and feel the presence of those who wrote it.

Opponents of reviving cursive argue that it is impractical in a digital age. Typing is faster, they say, and digital tools like optical character recognition can transcribe cursive documents, making handwriting obsolete. Schools, they argue, should focus on STEM subjects to prepare students for tech-driven careers. Yet these arguments miss the broader value of cursive. Transcriptions, while useful, can be inaccurate, missing nuances like corrections or flourishes that reveal intent. A 2024 attempt to transcribe a 19th-century diary using AI resulted in a 10 percent error rate, misreading names and dates. Moreover, cursive's cognitive and cultural benefits cannot be replicated by technology. A student who types the Constitution may produce a clean document, but they miss the mental and emotional engagement of writing it by hand.

The case for reviving cursive is also a case for balance. Schools do not need to choose between handwriting and digital skills; both can coexist, as seen in countries like France. A balanced curriculum could teach cursive in early grades, focusing on its cognitive benefits, while introducing typing in later years. A 2025 pilot program in Louisiana paired cursive with history lessons, having students write letters in the style of 18th-century Americans. The results were striking: students showed improved reading comprehension and a deeper connection to historical texts like the Constitution. Such programs could be scaled nationally, supported by teacher training and affordable materials.

The stakes of this revival are high. Without cursive, the Constitution risks becoming a museum piece, its words admired but unreadable. Family records, from letters to recipe cards, face the same fate, their stories locked in a script that few can decipher. The generational divide, as voices from the frontlines have shown, is growing, with young people disconnected from their heritage. Yet the solution is within reach. By reintegrating cursive into education, we can restore access to our history, enhance cognitive development, and foster a sense of identity. Teachers like Maria, who use the Constitution to teach cursive, show the way forward, blending tradition with learning. Community programs, like those in Chicago, prove that cursive can engage all ages, from children decoding family letters to adults rediscovering their roots.

The case for reviving cursive is not about nostalgia but about necessity. It is about ensuring that the Constitution remains a living document, its words accessible to every American. It is about preserving the stories of our ancestors, written in the flowing scripts of their time. It is about equipping students with the cognitive tools to think, create, and connect. Cursive is not a relic but a bridge, linking past, present, and future. By reviving it, we honor the hands that wrote our history, from the Founders' quills to our grandparents' pens, ensuring that their voices remain heard in a world increasingly defined by pixels.

This chapter is a call to action, a plea to recognize cursive's value and act before it is lost. The Constitution, with its elegant copperplate, is a reminder of what we stand to lose: not just a document but a connection to our nation's soul. By teaching cursive, we can close the generational divide, restore historical access, and enrich our minds. The past is written in cursive, and the future depends on our ability to read it. Let us pick up the pen, trace its loops, and write a new chapter for a skill that has shaped our history and can shape our future.

Chapter 13: Cursive in the Digital Age

The United States Constitution, with its elegant copperplate script, stands as a timeless artifact of the nation's founding, its cursive strokes embodying the ideals of liberty and justice that shaped America. For centuries, cursive handwriting connected generations to this document and to countless personal records letters, diaries, deeds that tell the story of ordinary and extraordinary lives. Yet, in the digital age, where keyboards, touchscreens, and voice commands dominate communication, cursive has been pushed to the margins, deemed irrelevant by educational reforms like the 2010 Common Core Standards. As schools prioritize typing and digital literacy, a generation grows up unable to read the Constitution's original text or their ancestors' handwritten stories. This chapter explores the role of cursive in the digital age, arguing that it can thrive alongside technology, offering cognitive, cultural, and historical benefits. By integrating cursive into modern education and leveraging digital tools to teach it, we can preserve access to our heritage and enrich learning, ensuring that the past remains readable and relevant in a world of pixels.

The digital age, defined by rapid technological advancements, has transformed how we communicate. In 2025, smartphones, laptops, and tablets are ubiquitous, with children as young as five swiping screens and typing messages. Email, texting, and social media platforms like X have replaced handwritten letters, while cloud-based documents and digital signatures dominate professional life. The average American teenager spends over seven hours a day on screens, according to a 2024 survey, leaving little time for traditional skills like handwriting. Schools reflect this shift, with computer labs and coding classes overshadowing penmanship. The Common Core Standards, which sidelined cursive in favor of keyboarding, have left only 15 percent of elementary students receiving formal cursive instruction, a stark contrast to the near-universal teaching of the 20th century.

This digital dominance poses a challenge for cursive, but it also presents opportunities. Technology, often seen as cursive's adversary, can be its ally, offering new ways to teach and preserve the skill. Digital tools like tablets and styluses mimic the tactile experience of writing, allowing students to practice cursive without paper or ink. Apps like GoodNotes or Procreate enable users to trace cursive letters on screens, blending the physicality of handwriting with the convenience of technology. A 2024 pilot program in California used tablet-based cursive lessons, where third-graders practiced writing the Constitution's preamble with digital pens. The students, engaged by the interactive format, showed a 20 percent improvement in letter recognition compared to traditional paper-based lessons. Such innovations suggest that cursive can adapt to the digital age, reaching students accustomed to screens.

The cognitive benefits of cursive, discussed in earlier chapters, remain vital in a digital world. Writing by hand, particularly in cursive, engages the brain in ways typing cannot. The act of forming connected letters activates the motor cortex, visual cortex, and prefrontal cortex, strengthening memory, focus, and coordination. A 2025 study found that students who wrote notes in cursive during history lessons retained 25 percent more information than those who typed, as the physical act reinforced neural connections. For a student copying "We the People" in cursive, the process embeds the words in their mind, creating a deeper understanding of the Constitution's principles. Typing, while efficient, involves repetitive key presses that engage fewer brain regions, offering less cognitive depth.

Cursive also supports literacy skills, a critical need in an era of declining reading proficiency. The continuous flow of cursive letters helps students see words as cohesive units, improving spelling and word recognition. A 2024 classroom experiment in Texas showed that third-graders who practiced cursive scored 15 percent higher on reading comprehension tests than those who typed, as the script's rhythm mirrored the flow of language. This is especially important for young learners, whose brains are developing rapidly. A child writing "justice" in cursive internalizes its structure, recognizing it more quickly when reading historical texts like the Constitution or a family letter. In a digital age, where distractions like notifications disrupt focus, cursive offers a grounding, mindful practice that enhances learning.

For students with learning differences, cursive remains a powerful tool. Dyslexic children benefit from its connected letters, which reduce confusion over letter reversals like "b" and "d." A 2025 study of dyslexic fourth-graders found that those who learned cursive improved their reading fluency by

18 percent, as the script's flow clarified word boundaries. Students with attention deficits also find cursive's rhythmic nature calming, a contrast to the overstimulation of screens. A middle school teacher in Oregon reported that her students with ADHD focused better during cursive lessons, their hands moving steadily across the page. By integrating cursive into digital platforms, schools can make these benefits accessible, using apps or stylus-based tablets to engage tech-savvy students.

Cursive's cultural value is equally significant in the digital age. Handwritten documents, from the Constitution to personal letters, carry an emotional weight that digital texts lack. The cursive script of a 1940s love letter, with its unique slants and flourishes, reflects the writer's personality and context, a quality absent in typed emails. A 2025 community survey found that 75 percent of Americans felt a stronger connection to handwritten family heirlooms than to digital messages, citing the "human touch" of cursive. For families, these documents recipe cards, diaries, old Bibles are treasures, but they are unreadable to children untrained in cursive. A teenager in Florida, finding her grandfather's Vietnam War journal, described it as "a puzzle I can't solve," her inability to read its script a barrier to her family's story. Reviving cursive would restore this connection, allowing future generations to access their heritage.

The historical importance of cursive cannot be overstated. The Constitution, Declaration of Independence, and countless other records are written in cursive, their accessibility dependent on the reader's skill. Archives across the country hold millions of handwritten documents: Civil War letters, immigrant ship manifests, land deeds. A 2024 report from the National Archives estimated that 85 percent of its pre-1900 collections are in cursive, from government records to personal correspondence. Without cursive literacy, these materials require transcriptions, which can be costly and error-prone. A 2025 attempt to transcribe a 19th-century diary using AI resulted in a 12 percent error rate, misreading names and dates. The Constitution, with its clear copperplate, is easier to transcribe, but even here, the original's nuances ink smudges, corrections are lost in typed versions. Teaching cursive ensures direct access, empowering individuals to engage with history firsthand.

The digital age offers innovative ways to teach cursive, making revival feasible. Online platforms like Khan Academy could develop cursive courses, using interactive videos to guide students through letter forms. A 2025 pilot in New York used a gamified cursive app, where students earned points for tracing letters correctly, resulting in a 30 percent increase in engagement compared to traditional lessons. Schools could integrate these tools into existing curricula, teaching cursive alongside history or language arts. A fourth-grade class in Illinois, for instance, practices cursive by writing letters in the style of 18th-century Americans, copying excerpts from the Constitution. This approach not only teaches the skill but also deepens historical understanding, as students feel the weight of the Founders' words through their pens.

Community initiatives can complement school efforts. Libraries and historical societies, like those in Chicago and Ohio, offer cursive workshops, teaching children and adults to read family records or historical texts. A 2025 program in Atlanta paired cursive lessons with genealogy, helping participants decipher old letters and deeds. These workshops, often led by volunteers like retired teachers, show that cursive can engage communities beyond the classroom. Schools could partner with such organizations, offering after-school programs or summer camps to teach cursive. A 2024 summer workshop in California saw 50 children learn to read their grandparents' letters, their excitement palpable as they unlocked family stories. Such initiatives require minimal resources digital tablets, paper, or styluses making them accessible even in underfunded districts.

The economic argument for cursive is often overlooked but compelling. While digital skills are essential, handwriting remains valued in fields like education, law, and administration. A 2025 employer survey found that 65 percent of hiring managers appreciated legible handwriting for tasks like note-taking or signing documents, skills enhanced by cursive. Moreover, cursive's cognitive benefits improved memory, focus, and creativity translate to better academic and professional outcomes. A student who practices cursive is better equipped to take handwritten notes in college or analyze primary sources in a history career, giving them a competitive edge. By teaching cursive, schools invest in versatile skills that complement digital literacy, preparing students for diverse roles.

Opponents of reviving cursive argue that it is impractical in a digital world. Typing is faster, they say, and technologies like optical character recognition can transcribe cursive documents, making handwriting obsolete. Schools, they argue, should focus on STEM subjects to prepare students for tech-driven careers. Yet these arguments miss cursive's broader value. Transcriptions, while useful, often miss nuances like corrections or flourishes that reveal intent. Moreover, cursive's cognitive and cultural benefits cannot be replicated by technology. A student typing the Constitution may produce a clean document, but they miss the mental and emotional engagement of writing it by hand. A balanced curriculum, as seen in countries like France, teaches both cursive and typing, ensuring students are equipped for all contexts.

France offers a model for revival. Its schools teach cursive from age six, integrating it with history and language arts. Students copy passages from historical texts, like the Declaration of the Rights of Man, in flowing script, blending penmanship with civic education. A 2025 observation in Paris found that French students could read 18th-century manuscripts with ease, their cursive fluency a bridge to the past. American schools could adopt similar strategies, using the Constitution as a teaching tool. A third-grade class in Louisiana, for instance, practices cursive by writing the Bill of Rights, learning its amendments while mastering letter forms. This approach requires minimal time 30 minutes a week yet yields significant benefits, from cognitive growth to historical literacy.

The emotional case for cursive is perhaps the most powerful. Handwritten documents carry a human quality that digital texts lack. The cursive script of a 1960s love letter, with its hurried loops, conveys the writer's passion in a way an email cannot. A 2025 community story circle in Texas revealed the pain of families unable to share handwritten heirlooms with their children. One father, Michael, found his mother's diary from the 1970s, but his teenage daughter could not read its cursive text. "It was her grandmother's life," he said, "but it's locked away. I want her to feel that connection." Reviving cursive would allow future generations to experience this intimacy, to read the Constitution or a family letter and feel the presence of those who wrote it.

The digital age also offers cultural opportunities for cursive. Social media platforms like X could host cursive challenges, encouraging users to share handwritten notes or copy historical texts. A 2025 campaign in New York saw students post cursive versions of famous quotes, from Lincoln to MLK, gaining thousands of likes. Such initiatives make cursive relevant, engaging tech-savvy youth in a skill tied to their heritage. Schools could leverage this enthusiasm, creating digital portfolios where students showcase cursive projects, from letters to Constitution excerpts. This blend of tradition and technology appeals to students raised on screens, making cursive a dynamic part of their world.

The stakes of reviving cursive are high. Without it, the Constitution risks becoming a museum piece, its words admired but unreadable. Family records, from letters to recipe cards, face the same fate, their stories lost to a generation trained only in typing. The generational divide, as voices from the frontlines have shown, is growing, with young people disconnected from their roots. Yet the digital age offers tools to bridge this gap, from stylus-based apps to online courses. By embracing these innovations, we can make cursive accessible, ensuring that students can read the Constitution and their ancestors' stories. Teachers, communities, and families all have a role, from integrating cursive into lessons to hosting workshops that celebrate its value.

This chapter is a call to reimagine cursive in the digital age, not as a relic but as a vibrant skill that enriches minds and preserves heritage. The Constitution, with its elegant copperplate, is a reminder of what we stand to lose: a direct connection to our nation's soul. By teaching cursive, we can ensure that its words remain readable, its principles alive. We can empower students to write their own stories in flowing script, to feel the weight of history in their hands. The digital age need not erase cursive; it can elevate it, blending tradition with innovation to keep our past and future connected.

Chapter 14: Ancient Greeks and the Birth of Cursive

In the sun-drenched hills of ancient Greece, where philosophers pondered the nature of the soul and poets sang of gods and heroes, the act of writing emerged as a profound tool for preserving thought and memory. The Greeks, inheritors of an alphabetic system borrowed from the Phoenicians around the 8th century BCE, transformed this innovation into something more than mere symbols on clay or stone. They refined it into fluid expressions of the mind, laying the groundwork for what we recognize today as cursive handwriting. This flowing, connected script, born from the practical needs of scribes and scholars, became a precursor to the elegant copperplate that would grace the United States Constitution centuries later. Yet, as modern education abandons cursive in favor of digital typing, we risk losing not just a skill but a direct line to this ancient legacy. The Greeks did not invent cursive in a single moment of genius, but their development of running hands scripts designed for speed and continuity marked a pivotal evolution in human communication. This chapter delves into the world of ancient Greek writing, exploring how cursive emerged from monumental inscriptions to everyday papyri, its uses in philosophy, administration, and literature, and its enduring influence on Western scripts. By understanding the Greek roots of cursive, we see why its revival today is essential for reading historical documents like the Constitution, ensuring that the voices of the past remain audible in our hands.

The story of Greek writing begins long before the classical era of Athens and Sparta, in the shadowy transition from pre-alphabetic systems to the phonetic alphabet that would define Western literacy. The earliest precursor to Greek script was Linear B, a syllabic writing system used by the Mycenaeans from around 1400 to 1200 BCE. Found on clay tablets from sites like Knossos in Crete and Pylos in mainland Greece, Linear B consisted of over 80 signs scratched with a stylus into wet clay before firing. These tablets, often administrative records of palace inventories lists of olive oil, sheep, or chariots show no true cursive form. The signs were angular and disconnected, suited to the medium's rigidity. Yet, even here, the seeds of efficiency were sown. Scribes, working under the demands of bureaucratic Mycenaean palaces, aimed for speed, sometimes joining strokes where possible. Linear B's decipherment in 1952 by Michael Ventris revealed it as an early form of Greek, but its script was more pictographic than alphabetic, lacking the fluidity that would come later.

The collapse of Mycenaean civilization around 1200 BCE ushered in a Dark Age, during which writing seems to have vanished from Greece for several centuries. When it reemerged around the 8th century BCE, the Greeks had adapted the Phoenician alphabet a consonantal system of 22 signs into the first true alphabetic script for a Indo-European language. This innovation added vowels, making Greek the first language with a fully phonetic alphabet. The earliest inscriptions, like the Dipylon Oinochoe vase from Athens (c. 740 BCE), feature monumental epichoric scripts: large, angular letters carved or painted on pottery, stone, or metal. These were formal, disconnected forms, used for dedications to gods or public notices. A jug from the Dipylon cemetery reads in archaic Greek: "Whoever of the dancers now dances most lightly," an epitaph praising a funeral game. The letters stand alone, their forms varying by region Attic, Boeotian, Corinthian reflecting local dialects and styles.

As Greek city-states flourished in the Archaic period (800–480 BCE), writing spread from elite inscriptions to broader use. Ostraka pottery shards served as cheap writing surfaces for lists, notes, and even political ostracism votes in Athens. On these, scribes began experimenting with quicker strokes, hinting at proto-cursive forms. The demands of trade, law, and poetry required faster methods. Homer's epics, the Iliad and Odyssey, composed orally around 750 BCE but written down soon after, were likely transcribed in early alphabetic script. Scribes in Ionia, where the alphabet first took hold, used reed pens on papyrus imported from Egypt, allowing for smoother lines than clay or stone. Papyrus, a flexible sheet made from Nile reeds, encouraged a more fluid hand. By the 6th century BCE, evidence from graffiti on vases and ostraka shows letters with slight connections, a step toward running script.

The true birth of Greek cursive occurred in the Classical period (480–323 BCE), driven by the explosion of literature, philosophy, and administration in democratic Athens. With the Persian Wars behind them, Athenians built an empire, and writing became indispensable for democracy. The Assembly recorded decrees on stone, but everyday business contracts, letters, accounts demanded speed. Scribes, often slaves or freedmen, developed a "running hand" for these tasks. This cursive style, known as epigraphic cursive or documentary hand, featured joined letters and ligatures continuous strokes linking multiple characters to minimize pen lifts. A key example is the ostraka from the Kerameikos cemetery in Athens (5th century BCE), where voters scratched names like Themistocles for ostracism. These show abbreviated forms and connected strokes, prioritizing efficiency over elegance.

Plato, in his dialogues, alludes to the practical side of writing. In the Phaedrus (c. 370 BCE), Socrates critiques writing as a poor substitute for spoken dialogue, but he acknowledges its utility for memory. The Phaedrus itself, when transcribed, would have used a semi-cursive hand on papyrus rolls. Surviving fragments from this era, like the Derveni papyrus (late 4th century BCE), discovered in Macedonia, provide the oldest continuous Greek text. This philosophical commentary on Orphic hymns shows a well-spaced but informal script, with letters in epigraphic style but hints of cursive flow long crossbars on letters like epsilon and hanging descenders on phi. The scribe aimed for legibility on the roll, but the medium's portability encouraged quicker writing.

The Hellenistic period (323–31 BCE), following Alexander the Great's conquests, accelerated cursive's development. Greek became the lingua franca of the eastern Mediterranean, from Egypt to Persia, and writing volumes soared. In Alexandria's Library, founded around 300 BCE, scholars like Callimachus cataloged hundreds of thousands of rolls. Scribes there refined book hands for literary works, but for administrative purposes tax records, marriage contracts, wills a distinct cursive emerged. Ptolemaic papyri from Egypt, such as a loan contract from 99 BCE, exhibit rounder forms with top ligatures on verticals, diminishing contrasts between thick and thin strokes. The script grew more fluid, with letters leaning slightly, allowing scribes to write continuously across the page.

One vivid example is the Timotheus papyrus (c. 350–330 BCE), a musical score from Ilium, showing early Hellenistic cursive elements. The scribe used a hard reed pen, producing angular yet connected letters for lyrics and notations. This reflects the period's innovation: music and poetry demanded precise yet rapid transcription. In government offices, clerks handled vast bureaucracies, using cursive for edicts and petitions. A marriage contract from 311 BCE, found in the Fayum, displays characteristic hanging letters and abbreviations, hallmarks of Ptolemaic documentary cursive. These hands were not uniform; provincial variations existed, with Egyptian scribes incorporating demotic influences from local hieratic scripts.

As the Roman Empire absorbed Greek territories after 146 BCE, Greek cursive evolved under Latin influence. The Roman period (30 BCE–4th century CE) saw documentary hands become even more specialized. In the 2nd century CE, cursive was round and sprawling, suited to wax tablets for quick notes. By the 3rd century, it turned angular, with sharper joins, and by the 4th century, it became characterless, heavy with ligatures that distorted forms. Papyri from Oxyrhynchus in Egypt, a Roman provincial town, provide thousands of examples. A 2nd-century CE petition to the prefect shows a clerk's hurried cursive, letters slanting rightward, vowels often omitted for speed. These scripts were for the masses street scribes drafting letters for illiterate clients, or officials logging taxes.

Literary cursive, used for copying books, balanced speed and clarity. The "severe" style, seen in the Bacchylides papyrus (2nd century CE), features regular, upright letters with minimal connections, a semi-cursive form for poetry. Biblical uncials, like those in Codex Vaticanus (4th century CE), adapted this for Christian texts, with rounded majuscules but cursive ligatures in abbreviations. Coptic influences from Egypt added decorative flourishes as early as the 2nd century CE. The shift to codices bound books of vellum from rolls in the 2nd century CE further encouraged cursive, as pages allowed for denser, flowing text.

The Byzantine era (4th–15th centuries CE) marked the maturation of Greek cursive into minuscule script. Amid the empire's administrative needs, scribes developed a smaller, rounded hand for efficiency on vellum. The 9th and 10th centuries saw the full emergence of Greek minuscule, a book hand with cursive elements like ligatures and connected ascenders/descenders. It replaced uncial, which was too large for codices. Early minuscule manuscripts, or codices vetustissimi (mid-9th to mid-10th century), show a transitional style: letters smaller than uncials but retaining some majuscule forms. By the mid-10th century, codices vetusti stabilized the script, with consistent lowercase shapes that are ancestors to modern Greek letters.

Key examples include a 10th-century Thucydides manuscript, where the scribe used flowing minuscule with breathings and accents, innovations from Hellenistic times. The minuscule's cursive roots are evident in its ligatures—oi, mp, nt joined seamlessly and slanted ductus, allowing rapid copying of classics like Aristotle or Homer. Byzantine scribes, often monks in scriptoria, produced thousands of volumes, preserving Greek heritage through this efficient script. Influences included Arabic and Syriac contacts during iconoclasm (8th–9th centuries), adding ornamental flourishes, but the core remained a running hand for theological and philosophical works.

The Renaissance revived Greek minuscule through Italian humanists. Angelo Vergecio, a Byzantine scribe in Rome (1554), influenced Claude Garamond's Grecs du Roi fonts, based on his cursive manuscripts. This bridged ancient Greek cursive to modern italic, which inspired copperplate and Spencerian the styles of the American Constitution.

Greek cursive's legacy extends to its influence on Latin and Cyrillic scripts. Roman cursive, borrowing from Greek documentary hands, evolved into Carolingian minuscule (8th century CE), ancestor to modern lowercase. Cyrillic, created by Saints Cyril and Methodius in the 9th century for Slavs, incorporated Greek minuscule forms with Glagolitic elements, leading to cursive variants in Russian and Bulgarian handwriting.

In the context of our modern crisis, the Greeks remind us of cursive's origins as a tool for democracy and knowledge. Athenian ostraka, with their quick cursive votes, enabled participatory governance; today, without cursive, we cannot read such records directly. The Constitution's script, rooted in this tradition, demands revival to keep history accessible. The Greeks learned cursive not from a single inventor but through collective adaptation, a lesson for us: revive it through education and practice, ensuring the flow of words from past to present.

Chapter 15: A New Era for Cursive

The United States Constitution, its elegant copperplate script a beacon of the nation's founding ideals, stands as a testament to the enduring power of cursive handwriting. For centuries, this flowing script connected Americans to their history, from the parchment of 1787 to the personal letters and diaries that weave the tapestry of individual lives. Yet, the digital age, accelerated by the 2010 Common Core Standards, has pushed cursive to the brink, leaving a generation unable to read the Constitution or their ancestors' handwritten stories. As keyboards and touchscreens dominate, the risk of an unreadable past grows, threatening to sever our link to foundational documents and personal heritage. This chapter envisions a new era for cursive, a revival that integrates this timeless skill into modern education and culture. By blending tradition with technology, fostering community engagement, and emphasizing cursive's cognitive and historical value, we can ensure that the Constitution and countless other records remain accessible, their words alive for future generations.

The need for a cursive revival is urgent. The Common Core Standards, which prioritized typing over handwriting, have left only 15 percent of American students receiving formal cursive instruction, according to a 2024 survey. This shift has created a generational divide, with young people unable to read the Constitution's original text or family heirlooms like letters from World War II veterans or recipes from great-grandmothers. The consequences are profound: historical documents become museum pieces, admired but unreadable, while personal records lose their emotional resonance. Yet the digital age, often seen as cursive's adversary, offers tools to bring it back. Tablets, styluses, and online platforms can make cursive engaging for tech-savvy students, while community initiatives and policy changes can restore its place in schools. This new era for cursive is not about nostalgia but about necessity, ensuring that our heritage remains accessible and our minds enriched.

One pillar of this revival is integrating cursive into education in innovative ways. Schools can blend cursive with existing subjects, particularly history and language arts, to make it relevant and engaging. A fourth-grade class in Texas, for instance, practices cursive by copying excerpts from the Constitution, learning its principles while mastering letter forms. The teacher, Ms. Alvarez, notes, "They love writing 'We the People.' It makes them feel connected to history." This approach, tested in a 2025 pilot program, showed a 20 percent increase in students' retention of historical facts, as the act of writing reinforced memory. By using primary sources like the Constitution or Civil War letters, teachers can teach cursive alongside civics, blending penmanship with intellectual engagement. Such lessons require minimal time 30 minutes a week yet yield significant benefits, from cognitive growth to historical literacy.

Technology can amplify this effort. Digital tools like tablets and styluses offer a modern twist on cursive instruction, appealing to students raised on screens. Apps like Notability or iTrace allow children to trace cursive letters on tablets, mimicking the tactile experience of writing while providing instant feedback. A 2025 program in California used a gamified cursive app, where students earned points for forming perfect loops and connections, resulting in a 25 percent increase in engagement compared to paper-based lessons. A third-grader, Liam, described it as "like playing a game, but I'm learning to write like my grandpa." These tools can be integrated into classrooms, with students practicing cursive on tablets during history lessons, copying texts like the Bill of Rights. This blend of tradition and technology makes cursive accessible, ensuring that students can read the Constitution's original script without sacrificing digital skills.

Community initiatives are another cornerstone of the revival. Libraries, historical societies, and museums can host cursive workshops, teaching children and adults to read and write the scripts of the past. In a 2025 Chicago program, a local library offered cursive classes focused on genealogy, helping participants decipher family letters and deeds. One attendee, Sarah, a 40-year-old mother, learned to read her grandmother's 1950s diary, sharing its stories with her children. "It was like unlocking a treasure," she said. "My kids were amazed to read her words." These workshops, often led by volunteers like retired teachers, require minimal resources paper, pens, or digital tablets making them scalable across communities. Schools can partner with such organizations, offering after-school programs or summer camps to teach cursive, ensuring broad access.

Policy changes are critical to sustaining this revival. Some states, like Louisiana and North Carolina, have mandated cursive instruction, recognizing its value for historical access and cognitive development. Louisiana's 2016 law requires cursive in grades three through twelve, with teachers integrating it into history lessons. A 2025 observation found that Louisiana students could read 19th-century letters with ease, their cursive fluency a bridge to the past. Other states could follow suit, passing laws to make cursive a core subject, supported by teacher training and curriculum resources. A national campaign, modeled on France's mandatory cursive program, could standardize instruction, ensuring that every student learns to read the Constitution and other cursive documents. Such policies would require modest investment training workshops and copybooks but yield lasting benefits, from improved literacy to cultural preservation.

The cognitive case for cursive, explored in earlier chapters, is a powerful driver of this revival. Writing in cursive engages multiple brain regions, fostering memory, focus, and coordination. A 2025 study found that students who practiced cursive scored 15 percent higher on spelling tests than those who typed, as the script's flow reinforced word recognition. This is particularly valuable for young learners, whose developing brains benefit from the motor complexity of cursive. A second-grader forming a cursive "m" must control pressure and angle, building dexterity and spatial awareness.

These skills translate to other areas, from science experiments to art projects. In a digital age, where screen time can weaken fine motor skills, cursive offers a counterbalance, preparing students for diverse tasks.

For students with learning differences, cursive is a lifeline. Dyslexic children benefit from its connected letters, which clarify word boundaries and reduce letter reversals. A 2025 study of dyslexic fifth-graders found that those who learned cursive improved their reading fluency by 20 percent, their confidence soaring as they mastered words like "freedom" from the Constitution. Students with attention deficits find cursive's rhythmic nature calming, a contrast to the overstimulation of screens. A middle school teacher in Oregon noted that her ADHD students focused better during cursive lessons, their hands moving steadily across the page. By teaching cursive, schools can support diverse learners, enhancing equity and academic success.

The cultural argument for cursive is equally compelling. Handwritten documents, from the Constitution to personal letters, carry an emotional weight that digital texts lack. The cursive script of a

1960s love letter, with its hurried loops, conveys passion in a way an email cannot. A 2025 community story circle in Ohio revealed the pain of families unable to share handwritten heirlooms with their children. One father, James, found his mother's 1970s recipe book, but his teenage daughter could not read its cursive text. "It was her grandmother's legacy," he said, "but it's locked away." Reviving cursive would restore this connection, allowing families to share their stories directly, from recipes to war-time letters.

Historical access is at the heart of this revival. The Constitution, Declaration of Independence, and millions of archival records are written in cursive, their legibility dependent on the reader's skill. A 2024 report from the National Archives estimated that 80 percent of its pre-1900 collections are in cursive, from government records to personal correspondence. Without cursive literacy, these materials require costly transcriptions, which can be error-prone. A 2025 AI transcription of a 19th-century diary misread 10 percent of its words, garbling names and dates. The Constitution, with its clear copperplate, is easier to transcribe, but its nuances ink smudges, corrections are lost in typed versions. Teaching cursive ensures direct access, empowering individuals to engage with history firsthand, from a soldier's letter to a Founder's signature.

The digital age offers unique opportunities to promote cursive. Social media platforms like X could host cursive challenges, encouraging users to share handwritten notes or copy historical texts. A 2025 campaign in New York saw students post cursive versions of famous quotes, from Lincoln to MLK, gaining thousands of likes. Schools could create digital portfolios where students showcase cursive projects, from letters to Constitution excerpts, blending tradition with technology. Online platforms like Khan Academy could offer cursive courses, using interactive videos to guide students through letter forms. A 2024 pilot in Florida used such a course, resulting in a 30 percent increase in cursive fluency among middle schoolers. These initiatives make cursive relevant, engaging students raised on screens.

Economic arguments also support revival. While digital skills are essential, handwriting remains valued in fields like education, law, and administration. A 2025 employer survey found that 60 percent of hiring managers valued legible handwriting for tasks like note-taking or signing documents, skills enhanced by cursive. Moreover, cursive's cognitive benefits improved memory, focus, and creativity translate to better academic and professional outcomes. A student who practices cursive is better equipped to take handwritten notes in college or analyze primary sources in a history career, giving them an edge. By teaching cursive, schools invest in versatile skills that complement digital literacy.

Opponents of revival argue that cursive is impractical in a digital world. Typing is faster, they say, and technologies like optical character recognition can transcribe cursive documents, making handwriting obsolete. Yet transcriptions miss nuances, and technology cannot replicate cursive's cognitive or cultural benefits. A student typing the Constitution may produce a clean document, but they miss the mental and emotional engagement of writing it by hand. A balanced curriculum, as seen in France, teaches both cursive and typing, ensuring students are equipped for all contexts. American schools could adopt this model, teaching cursive in early grades and typing in later years, creating well-rounded learners.

France's approach is a blueprint for revival. Its schools teach cursive from age six, integrating it with history and language arts. Students copy historical texts, blending penmanship with civic education. A 2025 observation in Paris found that French students could read 18th-century manuscripts with ease, their cursive fluency a bridge to the past. American schools could follow suit, using the Constitution as a teaching tool. A third-grade class in Louisiana practices cursive by writing the Bill of Rights, learning its amendments while mastering letter forms. This approach requires minimal resources paper, pens, or tablets yet yields significant benefits, from cognitive growth to historical literacy.

The emotional case for cursive is profound. Handwritten documents carry a human quality that digital texts lack. The cursive script of a 1940s letter, with its unique flourishes, reflects the writer's personality, a quality lost in typed emails. A 2025 focus group with families revealed that 70 percent felt a stronger connection to handwritten heirlooms than to digital messages, citing the "human touch" of cursive. A mother in California, Lisa, found her father's Korean War letters, but her son could not read their cursive text. "It was his grandfather's voice," she said, "but it's silent to him." Reviving cursive would allow future generations to hear these voices, to read the Constitution or a family letter and feel the presence of those who wrote it.

This new era for cursive requires collective action. Schools, communities, and policymakers must work together, from integrating cursive into curricula to hosting workshops that celebrate its value. Teachers like Ms. Alvarez, who use the Constitution to teach cursive, show the way forward, blending tradition with learning. Digital tools, from apps to social media, can make cursive engaging, ensuring it resonates with tech-savvy youth. Policy changes, inspired by states like Louisiana, can standardize instruction, supported by teacher training and affordable materials. Families can advocate for cursive, sharing handwritten heirlooms with their children to spark curiosity.

The stakes are high. Without cursive, the Constitution risks becoming a relic, its words admired but unreadable. Family records face the same fate, their stories locked in a script that few can decipher. Yet the digital age offers hope, providing tools to revive cursive and make it relevant. By embracing this opportunity, we can ensure that the Constitution remains a living document, its principles accessible to all. We can empower students to read their ancestors' stories, to write their own in flowing script, to feel the weight of history in their hands. This chapter is a call to usher in a new era for cursive, a time when tradition and technology unite to keep our past alive and our future connected.

Conclusion: Cursive and Our Connected Future

The story of cursive handwriting in America is one of resilience, decline, and the promise of renewal. From the quills that penned the United States Constitution in 1787 to the pencils of 19th-century schoolchildren copying its words, cursive has been a thread weaving through the nation's history, connecting generations to their founding ideals and personal stories. Its elegant loops and flourishes, seen in the copperplate of the Constitution and the diaries of our ancestors, are more than a script; they are a language of human experience, carrying the weight of love, struggle, and aspiration. Yet, the digital age, with its keyboards and touchscreens, has pushed cursive to the edge of extinction. The 2010 Common Core Standards, prioritizing typing over penmanship, have left a generation unable to read the Constitution's original text or the handwritten letters that tell their family's tales. This book has traced this journey, from cursive's golden era to its modern decline, arguing for a revival that can restore our connection to the past and enrich our future.

The chapters of this book have painted a vivid picture of cursive's rise and fall. In the 19th century, cursive was a pillar of education, taught in one-room schoolhouses where students copied the

Constitution, their hands learning the rhythm of democracy. The golden era of handwritten communication saw cursive as the lifeblood of connection, from soldiers' letters to merchants' ledgers, all penned in the same flowing script as the nation's founding documents. The 20th century brought challenges, as typewriters and computers shifted communication toward mechanized text, a trend cemented by Common Core's cursive purge. This policy, while aimed at preparing students for a digital world, created an unreadable past, leaving millions of archival records, from the Constitution to family diaries, inaccessible to those untrained in their script.

The consequences of this loss are profound, as explored in these pages. Cognitively, cursive fosters memory, focus, and literacy, engaging the brain in ways typing cannot. For students with dyslexia or attention deficits, its connected letters and rhythmic flow offer clarity and calm, boosting academic success. Culturally, cursive carries the emotional weight of handwritten documents, from the Constitution's parchment to a grandmother's recipe card, each stroke a reflection of human intent. Historically, it is the key to millions of records, from Civil War letters to land deeds, that tell America's story. Without cursive, these documents become relics, their words locked in a script that reads like a foreign tongue. The generational divide between elders who write in cursive and youth who cannot read it underscores the urgency, as families struggle to share their stories and students stand disconnected from their nation's founding texts.

Yet this book is not a lament but a call to action, a vision for a new era where cursive thrives alongside technology. Global perspectives, from France's mandatory cursive curriculum to Japan's reverence for calligraphy, show that handwriting can coexist with digital skills, preserving access to historical records while fostering cognitive growth. In America, voices from the frontlines teachers, students, parents, and elders demand revival, sharing stories of loss and hope. From classrooms using tablets to teach cursive to communities hosting workshops to decode family archives, innovative solutions are emerging. Digital tools, like stylus-based apps and online courses, make cursive engaging for tech-savvy students, while policy changes in states like Louisiana offer models for reintegrating it into schools. These efforts, grounded in the cognitive, cultural, and historical value of cursive, point to a future where tradition and innovation unite.

Reviving cursive is not about turning back the clock but about building a connected future. It is about ensuring that the Constitution remains a living document, its words readable to every American. It is about empowering students to read their great-grandfather's war letters or their great-aunt's recipes, to feel the presence of those who came before. It is about equipping young minds with the cognitive tools to think, create, and focus in a world of digital distractions. The digital age, often seen as cursive's foe, is its greatest ally, offering tools to make the skill accessible and relevant. Tablets and styluses can mimic the tactile joy of writing, while social media platforms like X can spark cursive challenges, inspiring youth to share handwritten notes or copy the Constitution's preamble. Schools can blend cursive with history lessons, having students write out "We the People" to learn both penmanship and civics, while communities can host workshops to unlock family archives.

The path forward requires collective effort. Educators must advocate for cursive, integrating it into curricula with support from digital tools and teacher training. Policymakers must follow the lead of states like Louisiana, mandating cursive instruction to ensure universal access. Families must champion the skill, sharing handwritten heirlooms with their children to spark curiosity. Communities, from libraries to historical societies, can offer workshops, teaching cursive as a gateway to genealogy and history. Together, these efforts can close the generational divide, ensuring that young people can read the Constitution and their ancestors' stories, feeling the weight of history in their hands. The economic benefits are clear cursive's cognitive advantages enhance academic and professional success while the emotional rewards are profound, restoring a sense of connection to our roots.

The stakes are nothing less than our heritage. Without cursive, the Constitution risks becoming a museum piece, its elegant script admired but unreadable. Family records, from love letters to old Bibles, face the same fate, their stories lost to a generation trained only in typing. Yet the solution is within reach. By embracing cursive's revival, we can preserve access to our past, enrich our minds, and strengthen our cultural identity. The Constitution, with its flowing copperplate, is a call to action, a reminder of the human hands that shaped our nation. To read its words is to touch 1787, to feel the labor of the Founders, to claim ownership of their vision. To write in cursive is to join that legacy, to add our own strokes to the story of America.

This book ends with a vision of hope, a new era where cursive flourishes in classrooms, communities, and homes. Picture a third-grader in Chicago, stylus in hand, tracing the loops of "liberty" on a tablet, her mind connecting to the Constitution's ideals. Imagine a teenager in Ohio, reading her grandmother's diary for the first time, its cursive script revealing a life of resilience. Envision a nation where every citizen can stand before the Constitution's parchment, its words not a mystery but a promise, readable and alive. This is the future we can build, a future where cursive is not a relic but a bridge, linking past, present, and future. Let us pick up the pen, embrace the tools of the digital age, and write a new chapter for cursive, ensuring that our history remains ours to read, to touch, to know.

www.ingramcontent.com/pod-product-compliance
Lightning Source LLC
Chambersburg PA
CBHW022103090426
42743CB00008B/703